D1500252

LYRICS

BY OSCAR HAMMERSTEIN II

SIMON AND SCHUSTER · NEW YORK

1949

LYRICS FROM

TO DOROTHY

"THE SONG IS YOU"

I have included in this collection only those lyrics which I wrote alone. This will account for the absence of several well-known songs like "Who?," "The Desert Song," "The Riff Song," "One Alone," "The Indian Love Call," and others from the plays *Sunny*, *The Desert Song*, *Rose Marie*, and *Wildflower*. The lyrics for all of these were written in collaboration with Otto Harbach.

Oscar Hammerstein, II

TABLE OF CONTENTS

SONGS WITH JEROME KERN

SHOW BOAT

MUSIC IN THE AIR

OTHER SONGS WITH JEROME KERN

SONGS WITH MUSIC BY GEORGES BIZET

CARMEN JONES

PREFACE

As though the pleasure and profit in writing the music for a great many of these songs were not enough, the composer now is granted the opportunity to say a few words by way of introducing this collection of Hammerstein lyrics. The composer, having some intimate knowledge of these particular words, is in the best possible position to say the best possible words concerning them and is willing and eager to do so.

The work of my collaborator and friend has been called poetry; it has been called light verse; it has even been called song-writing. It is possible that between the covers of some book there is better poetry than this. Perhaps there exist finer specimens of light versification, but there is not to be found anywhere else such a perfect collection of examples of the lyric-writer's art. It is to be hoped, then, that these words will be read for what they are: words for songs, and the best possible words.

It may be said that the music of songs is continually being played without the accompanying words; played on the radio and records or whistled in the street. This is not a fact. The words are inherently present in every performance of the tune, amateur or professional, if only in the title, for never does a song achieve any sort of public unless the words have at some point made a joint impact with the music on the individual and public ear. Once heard, the words, when they are good words, may be superficially forgotten but they are emotionally remembered. The old defensive and competitive cry of the composer, "Nobody whistles the words," is simply not true. It is obvious that no one since 1927 has ever given an "abstract" performance of the music of "Ol' Man River." With the music there has always been the river, the injustice, the pain, and the hope and fear of death. Every delivery boy whistles these things; because Mr. Kern and Mr. Hammerstein, people of high talent and deep feeling, achieved a noble work of collaboration.

Then, why this book? Why a permanent recording of the divorcement of one sort of talent from another? Simply because these lyrics are the best of their kind. It should be immensely rewarding to examine them out of context if only to discover their indispensability to the context itself. Perhaps if the reader sees the bare words "The corn is as high as a elephant's eye," and remembers that the proper music had to be provided for these words, he will gain some understanding not only of the problem posed the composer by the words but the solution of the composer's problem provided by the words *themselves. Again, there is an almost inevitable musical pathway leading from the words,*

> *"I'm as restless as a willow in a windstorm,*
> *I'm as jumpy as a puppet on a string."*

It's a lonesome girl singing. Therefore, the tune should be feminine, young, nervous, and, if possible, pretty like the girl.

It becomes apparent, then, that Hammerstein must be something of a musician to function well in his field, just as his composer should know something about words.

Of course, these are merely phases of technique in the examination of these words. The real validity for the publication of the book is that they are wonderful words, that they sing well of this country, and that they form a large and lasting part of our song heritage. It seems only fair that they be placed between covers for enlightenment and fun.

RICHARD RODGERS

LYRICS

BY OSCAR HAMMERSTEIN II

NOTES ON LYRICS

It took me years to learn that I did not play the piano very well. I so enjoyed my own playing. I tackled everything—Victor Herbert, Verdi, Leoncavallo, George Cohan. What expression I could put into their music! What exaltation I felt! My mother thought I had "a lovely touch," she told her friends. But when I became fifteen or sixteen my own friends began to express less sympathetic reactions, and it became clear to me that they were not hearing the same music I thought I was hearing when I played. Remembering this illuminating and disturbing experience, I have misgivings right now as I embark on a discussion of lyrics. I am going to love it, but will you? The hunter gloats reminiscently over the last saber-toothed tiger he has brought back alive. So does the songwriter like to tell of how he has captured a refrain and imprisoned it safely behind thirty-two bars. Both are likely to overrate the spare time of their audience.

One consideration encourages me. Almost every layman I have ever met exhibits a real curiosity about songs and how they are written. It is a standing joke among authors and composers that when they meet people the first question asked of them is, "Which comes first, the words or the music?" Perhaps it is high time that one of us stopped laughing at the classic query and provided a sensible answer to it. There is nothing foolish about the

3

question. A song is a wedding of two crafts, and it is a natural thing to wonder how they meet and live together. Feeling safe on the ground of an interest so frequently expressed, I will start these notes with this subject.

There is, as a matter of fact, no invariable or inevitable method for writing songs. Sometimes the words are written first, sometimes the music. Sometimes two or more collaborators lock themselves in a room and write words and music at the same time. The kind of songs, the individuals involved and the conditions under which they work dictate the process. Grand opera scores are almost always set to texts already written by the librettists. In the case of the most famous of all comic opera collaborations, it was the librettist, Gilbert, who wrote the words first. He would sometimes mail an entire act to Sullivan, who would then set music to his verses. On the other hand, the lyrics for most of the popular songs and musical comedies in our country today are written after the music. Up until my first collaboration with Richard Rodgers in 1943, I had always written this way. For twenty-five years, collaborating with Jerome Kern, Herbert Stothart, Sigmund Romberg, Rudolf Friml and Vincent Youmans, I set words to their music. It would seem to most people —and I am one of them—that writing the words first would be a more logical procedure, music being the more flexible and less specific of the two mediums. Why then did I write in this upside-down manner for so long a time? And why do most other writers in our country today continue to write in this way?

In the first decade of this century there were two factors which led songwriters into the custom of writing words to music. The best musical plays of that time were being created in Vienna. When they were imported, American librettists had to write translations and adaptations for melodies that had been set to another language. In those days we imported not only plays from Middle Europe. Many of the composers themselves came over here, settled down and became American citizens. They embraced our democratic philosophy, but they found it much more difficult to get used to our language. Lyric writers who submitted verses to be set were horrified by the abortive accents written to their words, and they soon found it less trying on their nerves to let the foreign musician have his say first and then write a lyric to fit his melody.

The second influence was not foreign at all. It was distinctly an American one—the broken rhythm. First came ragtime, then jazz. For the purpose of creating these eccentric deviations from orthodox meters, it was better to let the composer have his head. Concomitant with these new rhythms came what we called, in 1911, "the dance craze." Dancing, once confined to ballrooms and performed mainly by the young, became a new international sport indulged in by all people of all ages in all kinds of restaurants and at all meal times, lunch, tea, dinner and supper. The hit melodies of that time had to be good dance melodies. This being the most important consideration, it was better for the lyric writer

5

to trail along after the composer and fit his words to a refrain written mainly to be danced to. Many lyrics of the period were about dancing. Irving Berlin wrote "Everybody's Doing It." (Doing what? The turkey trot!) People were also, in other songs, doing the bunny hug and the grizzly bear. Not satisfied with writing lyrics describing dances already established by leading teachers and famous dancing teams, lyric writers set to work creating dances, giving them names, and hoping that the public would follow them. (This tendency persisted and went into the twenties, when numbers like "Bambalina" and "The Varsity Drag" were urged upon the public by songwriters. It continued into the sound movies of the thirties. "The Carioca" and "The Continental" were names given by lyric writers to dances, and Fred Astaire and Ginger Rogers illustrated them for us. We have been told also what a treat it is to beat our feet on the Mississippi mud, and not long ago "The Jersey Bounce" was recommended to us as a constant exercise. Even as I write these notes we are being warned on the radio that if we don't do "The Hucklebuck" we will be out of luck.)

I have conducted no exhaustive investigation of this subject, but these developments, as I remember them, seem to have been the chief influences which established the American songwriter's habit of writing the music first and the words later. It is a strange habit, an illogical one, but not entirely without compensating virtues. Writing in this way, I have frequently fallen into the debt of my composers for words and ideas that might never

6

have occurred to me had they not been suggested by music. If one has a feeling for music—and anyone who wants to write lyrics had better have this feeling—the repeated playing of a melody may create a mood or start a train of thought that results in an unusual lyric. Words written in this way are likely to conform to the spirit of the music. It is difficult to fit words into the rigid framework of a composer's meter, but this very confinement might also force an author into the concise eloquence which is the very essence of poetry. There is in all art a fine balance between the benefits of confinement and the benefits of freedom. An artist who is too fond of freedom is likely to be obscure in his expression. One who is too much a slave to form is likely to cripple his substance. Both extremes should be avoided, and no invariable laws or methods should be obeyed. In our collaboration Mr. Rodgers and I have no definite policy except one of complete flexibility. We write songs in whatever way seems best for the subject with which we are dealing, and the purposes of the song in the story which we are telling. Most often I write the words first, and yet in nearly all of our scores there are at least one or two songs in which he wrote the music first. When we first started to write together in 1943, we had no conversations on method. The first song we wrote was "Oh, What a Beautiful Mornin'," and the words were written first. I would like to tell you how this happened, because it furnishes a typical illustration of composer-author collaboration in the structure of a musical play.

Attacking the job of turning Lynn Riggs' *Green Grow the Lilacs* into what eventually became *Oklahoma!*, the first serious problem that faced us involved a conflict of dramaturgy with showmanship. As we planned our version, the story we had to tell in the first part of the first act did not call for the use of a female ensemble. The traditions of musical comedy, however, demand that not too long after the rise of the curtain the audience should be treated to one of musical comedy's most attractive assets—the sight of pretty girls in pretty clothes moving about the stage, the sound of their vital young voices supporting the principals in their songs. Dick and I, for several days, sought ways and means of logically introducing a group of girls into the early action of the play. The boys were no problem. Here was a farm in Oklahoma with ranches nearby. Farmers and cowboys belonged there, but girls in groups? No. Strawberry festivals? Quilting parties? Corny devices! After trying everything we could think of, and rejecting each other's ideas as fast as they were submitted, after passing through phases during which we would stare silently at each other unable to think of anything at all, we came finally to an extraordinary decision. We agreed to start our story in the real and natural way in which it seemed to want to be told! This decision meant that the first act would be half over before a female chorus would make its entrance. We realized that such a course was experimental, amounting almost to the breach of an implied contract with a musical comedy audience. I cannot say truthfully that we were

8

worried by the risk. Once we had made the decision, everything seemed to work right and we had that inner confidence people feel when they have adopted the direct and honest approach to a problem.

Now, having met our difficulty by simply refusing to recognize its existence, we were ready to go ahead with the actual writing. We had agreed that we should start the play outside a farmhouse. The only character on the stage would be a middle-aged woman sitting at a butter churn. The voice of Curly, a cowboy, would be heard off-stage, singing. Searching for a subject for Curly to sing about, I recalled how deeply I had been impressed by Lynn Riggs' description at the start of his play.

> "It is a radiant summer morning several years ago, the kind of morning which, enveloping the shapes of earth—men, cattle in the meadow, blades of the young corn, streams—makes them seem to exist now for the first time, their images giving off a visible golden emanation that is partly true and partly a trick of imagination, focusing to keep alive a loveliness that may pass away."

On first reading these words, I had thought what a pity it was to waste them on stage directions. Only readers could enjoy them. An audience would never hear them. Yet, if they did, how quickly they would slip into the mood of the story. Remembering this reaction, I reread the description and determined to put it into song. "Oh, What a Beautiful Mornin'" opens the play and

9

creates an atmosphere of relaxation and peace and tenderness. It introduces the light-hearted young man who is the center of the story. My indebtedness to Mr. Riggs' description is obvious. The cattle and the corn and the golden haze on the meadow are all there. I added some observations of my own based on my experience with beautiful mornings, and I brought the words down to the more primitive poetic level of Curly's character. He is, after all, just a cowboy and not a playwright.

"The corn is as high as a elephant's eye"—I first wrote "cow pony's eye." Then I walked over to my neighbor's cornfield and found that although it was only the end of August, the corn had grown much higher than that. "Cow pony" was more indigenous to the western background, but I had reservations about it even before I gauged the height of the corn. It reads better than it sounds. Sing "cow pony" to yourself and try to imagine hearing it for the first time in a song. It would be hard for the ear to catch.

"All the cattle are standin' like statues." This picture had come into my brain several years before I wrote the song, and it had stayed there quietly waiting to be used. When I came to the second verse of "Oh, What a Beautiful Mornin' " I remembered it. I remembered sitting on a porch in Pennsylvania one summer's day, watching a herd of cows standing on a hillside about half a mile away. It was very hot and there was no motion in the world. I suddenly found myself doing what I had never done before and have never done since. I was thinking up lines for a poem to describe what I saw. It was not to be used in a play, not to be set to music. I got this far with it:

> "The breeze steps aside
> To let the day pass.
> The cows on the hill
> Are as still as the grass."

I never wrote the lines on paper, nor did I ever do any work to polish them, nor did I extend the poem any further. Perhaps I was called to the phone, or perhaps I was infected with the laziness of an inactive landscape. But those cows on the hill "as still as the grass" were crystal‑lized in my memory by the words I had quite idly and casually composed, and up they came several years later to inspire me when I needed them.

Inspire me? Do authors write from inspiration? This is another bromidic question asked so frequently that I think it deserves a brief parenthesis at this point in my discussion of songs.

Any professional author will scoff at the implication that he spends his time hoping and waiting for a magic spark to start him off. There are few accidents of this kind in writing. A sudden beam of moonlight, or a thrush you have just heard, or a girl you have just kissed, or a beautiful view through your study window is seldom the source of an urge to put words on paper. Such pleasant experiences are likely to obstruct and delay a writer's work.

The legend of inspiration is, however, not a completely

silly one. If we broaden the base of the word and let it include the stored-up memories of the writer's emotional reactions, then inspiration figures very largely in what he puts down on paper. I suppose that every worth-while work is inspired by what has been seen or thought or felt by the writer at another time. Most bad fictional writing is the result of ignoring one's own experiences and contriving spurious emotions for spurious characters.

A term like "inspiration" annoys a professional author because it implies, in its common conception, that ideas and words are born in his brain as gifts from heaven and without effort. All who write know that writing is very, very hard work. Most of us do some work every day. Some get up early in the morning, as I do, and go straight to their studies as other men go to their business offices. Some writers prefer working at night and work very late, but all of us are trying to write something nearly all the time. Nobody waits to be inspired. Some days the work comes easier than other days, but you keep going because the chances of getting good ideas are more likely while you are trying to get them than when you are doing nothing at all.

To extend this already long "parenthesis" on inspiration, I submit another interesting illustration. About six years ago I attended the première of a musical play called *One Touch of Venus*, starring Mary Martin. In this play Mary portrayed the role of a kind of dream goddess, statuesque, romantic and very lovely indeed. In the last scene, however, she came on the stage transformed into the ideal desired by her lover. She wore a simple gingham dress. I turned to my wife and said, "There is a part she should play some day. She has been wonderful as 'Venus,' but here is the real Mary Martin, a little corn-fed girl from Texas." Today she is playing that part—a corn-fed girl from Arkansas named Nellie Forbush, invented by James Michener in his *Tales of the South Pacific*. When I started to write "I'm in Love With a Wonderful Guy," the picture of Mary in the gingham dress, entering in the last scene of *One Touch of Venus* six years ago, came into my mind and the first line of the refrain, "I'm as corny as Kansas in August," is a result of that memory. I could have said "as corny as Texas," where Mary came from, or I could have said "as corny as Arkansas," where the character Nellie Forbush came from, but for the purposes of singing, "as corny as Kansas" is a much better line because of the two "k" sounds and the alliteration created thereby, and because Kansas is a state more naturally associated with corn than the other two. End of parenthesis!

If you can remember that far back, I was discussing why and how songs are put into musical plays. Let us take a case where the music was written first. The refrain of "People Will Say We're in Love" was a melody written by Richard Rodgers with the thought that it might serve well as a duet for the two lovers in *Oklahoma!* This procedure is the more usual approach to writing musical comedy scores. The composer dreams up some melodies which suggest certain treatments. One might seem to

13

him to be the love duet of the piece, the other a good comedy song or a good tune to dance to. Almost all composers have a reservoir of melodies which come to them at different times and which they write down in what they call a sketchbook. When they start work on a new musical play, they play over these previously written melodies for their collaborator, and it is decided which ones can be used in this particular score. They then write additional melodies as required. Dick Rodgers, however, does not work in this way. He writes music only for a specific purpose. Ideas for tunes seldom come to him while he is walking down the street or riding in taxicabs, and he doesn't rush to his piano very often to write a tune just for the sake of writing a tune. I don't believe that either Dick or I would be very successful essentially as popular songwriters—writers of songs detached from plays. We can write words and music best when they are required by a situation or a characterization in a story.

The problem of a duet for the lovers in *Oklahoma!* seemed insurmountable. While it is obvious almost from the rise of the curtain that Curly and Laurey are in love with each other, there is also a violent antagonism between them, caused mainly by Laurey's youthful shyness, which she disguises by pretending not to care for Curly. This does not go down very well with him, and he fights back. Since this mood was to dominate their scenes down into the second act, it seemed impossible for us to write a song that said "I love you," and remain consistent with the attitude they had adopted toward each other. After talking this over for a long time, Dick and I hit upon the idea of having the lovers warn each other against any show of tenderness lest other people think they were in love. Of course, while they say all those things, they are obliquely confessing their mutual affection. Hence the title, "People Will Say We're in Love."

In all I have been saying, it will be noted that the composer and author work in very close collaboration during the planning of a song and the story that contains the song. This is an important point. It must be understood that the musician is just as much an author as the man who writes the words. He expresses the story in his medium just as the librettist expresses the story in his. Or, more accurately, they weld their two crafts and two kinds of talent into a single expression. This is the great secret of the well-integrated musical play. It is not so much a method as a state of mind, or rather a state for two minds, an attitude of unity. Musical plays, then, are not "books" written by an author with songs later inserted by a composer and a lyric writer. They are often written this way, but it is not a good way to write them and such plays seldom have a very long life. They are sure to lack form, and they cannot sustain a story interest when it is interrupted continually by songs that are of little value to the plot.

Dick and I stay very close together while drawing up the blueprint of a play. Before we start to put words or notes on paper we have agreed on a very definite and complete outline, and we have decided how much of the

15

story shall be told in dialogue and how much in song. We try to use music as much as we can. (We know, on the other hand, that certain subject matters are not good to be sung. If a character is calling up an airport and trying to reserve two seats on a plane and asking how much they are and what time the plane leaves, this is not good lyric or musical material. In grand opera, however, this would be sung in recitative or incorporated into an actual aria. I do not believe the American public will ever accept this kind of convention in its own language. When composers and librettists try to write what they call American operas and include the singing of passages like these, they are really not writing American operas at all. They are writing European operas governed by European traditions. That is one reason why such efforts have never been successful.)

After we have passed the blueprint stage, we then work together on the interior problems. We approach the spots we have chosen for songs and we discuss each song very carefully. It is not at all unlikely that Dick will give me valuable lyric ideas and I, on the other hand, frequently contribute important suggestions for the music. I don't mean to imply that I give him ideas for melodies. I have no melodic gift whatever, but I have a feeling for the treatment of a score, ideas for its structure.

One of the most helpful features of these periods of collaboration is the quick reaction you can get from your collaborator which helps you throw out bad ideas quickly and sustains your confidence in good ideas so that you go

16

ahead. I remember particularly one afternoon when Dick and I were working on the score of the motion picture, *State Fair*. As the story opens, the young girl is unhappy. She is not in love with anybody. She is going to a state fair with her family, but is not looking forward to it. She has the blues. She doesn't know why. It occurred to me that her feeling was very much like spring fever. It then occurred to me, very unhappily, that all state fairs are held in the autumn, September or early October. Then, wanting desperately to write a song about spring fever, I toyed with the notion of having her say, in effect, "It's autumn, but I have spring fever so 'it might as well be spring.'" Rather half-heartedly I threw the idea at Dick. He jumped up excitedly and said, "That's it." And from then on, that was it. All my doubts were gone. I had a partner behind me. In about a week I had written a refrain to this title. An hour after I gave the lyric to Dick he had set the melody. This is the annoying part of our collaboration. It takes me a week, and sometimes three weeks, to write the words of a song. After I give them to him it takes him an hour or two and his work is over. He responds remarkably to words, and when he likes them they immediately suggest tunes to him.

Two other songs in *Oklahoma!* are good illustrations of the dramatic part played by music in telling a story or depicting a character. Jud Fry worried us. A sulky farmhand, a "bullet-colored, growly man," a collector of dirty pictures, he frightened Laurey by walking in the shadow of a tree beneath her window every night. He

17

was heavy fare for a musical play. Yet his elimination was not to be considered because the drama he provided was the element that prevented this light lyric idyl from being so lyric and so idyllic that a modern theater audience might have been made sleepy, if not nauseous, by it. It was quite obvious that Jud was the bass fiddle that gave body to the orchestration of the story. The question was how to make him acceptable, not too much a deep-dyed villain, a scenery chewer, an unmotivated purveyor of arbitrary evil. We didn't want to resort to the boring device of having two other characters discuss him and give the audience a psychological analysis. Even if this were dramatically desirable, there are no characters in this story who are bright enough or well educated enough to do this. So we solved the problem with two songs, "Pore Jud" and "Lonely Room." They are both sung in the smokehouse set, the dingy hole where Jud lives, with no companions but a mouse who nibbles on a broom and a gallery of *Police Gazette* pictures on the walls—a most unpromising background from a musical standpoint.

In "Pore Jud," Curly, after suggesting to him how easy it would be for Jud to hang himself by a lasso from a rafter, goes on to describe what his funeral would be like. Unwelcome as the idea seems at first, Jud finds some features not unattractive to speculate on—the excitement he would cause by the gesture of suicide, the people who would come from miles around to weep and moan, especially the "womern" that had "tuk a shine" to Jud when he was alive. Jud is incredulous about these, but Curly points out that they "never come right out and show you how they feel, less'n you die first," and Jud allows that there's something in that theory. He becomes then, for a while, not just wicked, but a comic figure flattered by the attentions he might receive if he were dead. He becomes also a pathetic figure, pathetically lonely for attentions he has never received while alive. The audience begins to feel some sympathy for him, some understanding of him as a man.

In the second song, "Lonely Room," he paints a savage picture of his solitary life, his hatred of Curly and his mad desire for Laurey. This is a self-analysis, but it is emotional and not cerebral. No dialogue could do this dramatic job as vividly and quickly as does the song. When Lynn Riggs attended a rehearsal of *Oklahoma!* for the first time, I asked him if he approved of this number. He said, "I certainly do. It will scare hell out of the audience." That is exactly what it was designed to do.

There are few things in life of which I am certain, but I am sure of this one thing, that the song is the servant of the play, that it is wrong to write first what you think is an attractive song and then try to wedge it into a story.

Let me say a few words now about the actual writing of lyrics once the subject matter of the song has been determined, and once it has been placed in its proper spot in the telling of the story. I am often asked if I use a rhyming dictionary. I do. I find it a great help and a time saver. The one I like best is Loring's *Rhymer's Lexicon.*

A rhyming dictionary, however, should be used as a supplement to one's own ingenuity, and not a substitute for it. I do not open mine until I have exhausted my own memory and invention of rhymes for a word. Attractive combinations of words to make double and triple rhymes are not found in rhyming dictionaries, nor are modern words or colloquialisms which can be used with humorous effect in a song. A rhyming dictionary is of little use and may, in fact, be a handicap when one is writing a song which makes a feature of rhyming. If you would achieve the rhyming grace and facility of W. S. Gilbert or Lorenz Hart, my advice would be never to open a rhyming dictionary. Don't even own one. While I, on occasion, place a timid, encroaching foot on the territory of these two masters, I never carry my invasion very far. I would not stand a chance with either of them in the field of brilliant light verse. I admire them and envy them their fluidity and humor, but I refuse to compete with them. Aside from my shortcomings as a wit and rhymester — or, perhaps, because of them — my inclinations lead me to a more primitive type of lyric. The longer I write, the more interested I become in expressing my own true convictions and feelings in the songs I write. When I was very much younger, I thought that if ever I made all the money I needed out of writing musical comedy, I would then sit back and turn to straight dramatic plays in which I could say whatever I wanted to say and state my reactions to the world I live in. Later on, however, I became convinced that whatever I wanted to say could be said in songs, that I was not confined necessarily to trite or light subjects, and that since my talent and training in the writing of lyrics is far beyond my attainments in other fields of writing, I had better use this medium.

If one has fundamental things to say in a song, the rhyming becomes a question of deft balancing. A rhyme should be unassertive, never standing out too noticeably. It should, on the other hand, not be a rhyme heard in a hundred other popular songs of the time, so familiar that the listener can anticipate it before it is sung. There should not be too many rhymes. In fact, a rhyme should appear only where it is absolutely demanded to keep the pattern of the music. If a listener is made rhyme-conscious, his interest may be diverted from the story of the song. If, on the other hand, you keep him waiting for a rhyme, he is more likely to listen to the meaning of the words. A good illustration is "Ol' Man River." Consider the first part of the refrain:

> "Ol' Man River,
>   Dat Ol' Man River,
>   He mus' know sumpin'
>   But don' say nuthin',
>   He jes' keeps rollin',
>   He keeps on rollin' along.
>   He don' plant 'taters,
>   He don' plant cotton,
>   An' dem dat plants 'em
>   Is soon forgotten."

"Cotton" and "forgotten" are the first two words that rhyme. Other words are repeated for the sake of musical continuity and design. The same idea could be set to this music with many more rhymes. "River," instead of being repeated in the second line, could have had a rhyme— "shiver," "quiver," etc. The next two lines could have rhymed with the first two, the "iver" sounds continuing, or they could have had two new words rhyming with each other. I do not believe that in this way I could have commanded the same attention and respect from a listener, nor would a singer be so likely to concentrate on the meaning of the words. There are, of course, compensations for lack of rhyme. I've already mentioned repetition. There is also the trick of matching up words. "He mus' know sumpin' But don' say nuthin'." "Sumpin'" and "nuthin'" do not rhyme, but the two words are related. "He don' plant 'taters, He don' plant cotton." These two lines also match and complement each other to make up for the lack of a rhyme. Here is a song sung by a character who is a rugged and untutored philosopher. It is a song of resignation with a protest implied. Brilliant and frequent rhyming would diminish its importance.

Take, as a contrast, the refrain of "I'm in Love With a Wonderful Guy" from *South Pacific*. You will find in it interior rhymes, undemanded rhymes and light-hearted similes. The emotion expressed in this song is so simple that it can afford to wear the decorations and embroidery of more ingenious rhyming. There is no subtle philosophy involved. A girl is in love and her heart is sailing. She is sentimental and exuberant and triumphant in the discovery. The job of the lyric is to capture her spirit. I think it does. I am very fond of this song.

After rhyming, I would place next in importance a study and appreciation of phonetics. Some words and groups of words that look beautiful in printed poetry are unavailable to one who is writing lyrics to be sung to music. There is an inexorable mathematics in music — so many measures in a refrain, so many beats in a measure, and they cannot be ignored. There is rhythm and tempo, and its continuity must be unbroken. The concessions with which a melody can favor words are limited. The larynxes of singers are limited. They must be given a chance to breathe after a certain number of words have been sung, and if they are building up to a high note at the finish, they must be given a good deep breath before they attack it. Both the lyric writer and the composer must worry about all these things. If a song is not singable, it is no song at all.

The job of the poet is to find the right word in the right place, the word with the exact meaning and the highest quality of beauty or power. The lyric writer must find this word too, but it must be also a word that is clear when sung and not too difficult for the singer to sing on that note which he hits when he sings it. Wherever there are vocal climaxes and high notes, singers are comfortable only with vowels of an open sound. A word like "sweet," for instance, would be a very bad word on which to sing a high note. The "e" sound closes the larynx and the

23

singer cannot let go with his full voice. Furthermore, the "t" ending the word is a hard consonant which would cut the singer off and thwart his and the composer's desire to sustain the note. Now and then, when a lyric writer finds a word to which he is very attached, he tries to side-track these rules. He may say, "I don't care how many 's's' there are in this line, this is what I want to say and the singer will just have to slow up and sing very distinctly"; or he may say, "I don't care if that word does end with a hard consonant [like the 't' in 'sweet'], that is the only word I can use there and the singer will have to make the best of it." This kind of temperamental defiance is self-defeating because no word, however fine and lofty and exact its meaning may be, is a good word in a song if it is difficult to sing.

Dick Rodgers and I wrote a song, "What's the Use of Wond'rin'?" for *Carousel*. A great many people admired it and many of them have asked me why it was not more popular. Within the framework of the play it performed a dramatic service, but it was not sung a great deal on the radio, nor did it sell many copies or many phonograph records, and these factors are the modern measure of a song's popularity. I believe "What's the Use of Wond'rin'?" was severely handicapped because of the final word, "talk." The trouble with this word is the hard "k" sound at the end of it. The last two lines of the refrain are, "You're his girl and he's your feller, And all the rest is talk." This is exactly what I wanted the character to say. She is not a very well-educated girl, nor is she a subtle philosopher. Discussing the unpredictable, fascinating and sometimes brutal man with whom she is in love, she says in the song: What's the use of wond'rin' if the man you love is good or bad, or whether you like the way he wears his hat, or whether you ought to leave him or not, he's just the way he is and he can't be any different, and he has certain things given him by fate, and one of those things is you, and so whenever he wants you, you will go to him. After all, "you're his girl and he's your feller and all the rest is talk." I realized that I was defying convention in ending with the word "talk," but I had a perverse desire to try it anyway. Now, every once in a while you should try to break rules, to test them and see if, indeed, they are breakable. Sometimes you succeed and this is the way the most exciting things in the theater are done. Sometimes you fail. This time a good and sound rule slapped me down. I will not break it again. I believe that this song might have been very successful outside of the play had I finished it on an open vowel instead of a hard consonant. Suppose, for instance, the last line had been: "You're his girl and he's your feller — that's all you need to know." The singer could have hit the "o" vowel and held it as long as she wanted to, eventually pulling applause on it. (There is nothing wrong with pulling applause. No matter how much an audience enjoys a song, it likes to be cued into applause. It likes to be given a punctuation which says, "There, now it's over and we've given you our all, and now is exactly the right time for you to show your appreciation.")

One of the best examples of good singing endings in this book is the last line of "All the Things You Are": "When all the things you are, are mine." The singer opens his mouth wide to sing the word "are," and it is still open and he can give still more when he sings the second "are" right after it. It is true that the very last word ends in a consonant, but it is a soft consonant. Furthermore, the two notes that are hit by the repetition of the word "are" constitute the climax of the line, and the word "mine" becomes a sort of denouement.

All these last lines are good for singing: "Oh, what a beautiful day," "You'll never walk alone," "Once you have found her, never let her go," "Ol' Man River, he jes' keeps rollin' along," "Bali Ha'i, Bali Ha'i, Bali Ha'i." Try these out yourself, when you are taking your shower, and see how easily and effortlessly they roll out and up to the bathroom ceiling. In all cases you will find open vowels used and no hard consonants on high notes. The rule is not, of course, invariable and you will find freak endings, falsetto endings and dramatic endings, wherein the composer and the singer humor the line so that it can be sung without recourse to a conventional vocal climax. The last line, "The surrey with the fringe on the top" is a case in point. "Fringe" would seem an unpromising singing word, but somehow it sings very well. There is a softness to the "g" sound and although the vowel, a short "i," is a closed one, the singer usually takes it falsetto. In this case, it would be wrong for the composer to have written a dramatically vocal finish to a song so naïve and charming. The success of this unconventional musical and lyrical finish explains our temerity in breaking the rule in the case of "What's the Use of Wond'rin'?" but there we failed and with the other song we succeeded.

Stressing as I have the story functions of songs in musical plays, why am I concerned with their reception outside the show? Mainly because a songwriter wants, more than anything, to hear his songs sung by as many people as possible for as long a time as possible. A great many compositions which achieve temporary popularity on the radio are shallow and trivial, but every song that has a long life says something fundamental, and says it in an attractive way musically and lyrically. Every song of this kind requires little effort to sing or to listen to. A song that requires little effort to sing or to listen to is usually the result of great effort on the part of its creators.

Lest, at any point, I seem to be laying down rigid rules, let me acknowledge quickly that there are no such things in my craft. Some of our most successful compositions stray far beyond the narrow borders that restrict the well-made refrain. "Star Dust" rambles and roams like a truant schoolboy in a meadow. Its structure is loose, its pattern complex. Yet it has attained the kind of long-lived popularity that few songs can claim. What has it got? I'm not certain. I know only that it is beautiful and I like to hear it. It is a mood-creating song. It has repose and wistfulness. It is something very special, all by itself. Anyone who tried to imitate it would be a fool.

"Begin the Beguine" is another rule-breaker — too long! It is what is known among professional songwriters as "a tape worm." It hasn't the cohesive and compact continuity of a popular song. But it *is* popular and has been for about twenty years. That's *very* popular. This is an "atmospheric" song. It transports you to places where palm trees wave across yellow moons and Spanish is spoken, which is exactly what Mr. Porter wants it to do to you.

Songs like these, ignoring the orthodox principles, are freaks and anomalies. One doesn't learn much from anomalies. Common-sense solutions to normal problems are the first things to master. One very fundamental problem is the special use of certain words in songs. Some words, for instance, have lost their value through overuse. "Divine" is such a word. It occurs in "All the Things You Are." I didn't like this word when I submitted the song to Jerry Kern and, as I had anticipated, he didn't like it either. For many days I worked, trying to find a substitute. I just couldn't. The last lines are: "Some day I'll know that moment divine, When all the things you are, are mine." I was trapped. "All the things you are," referred to poetically and romantically throughout the song, are certainly what I wish to be "mine." I could not surrender this finish. But it demands an "ine" rhyme. "Some day I'll know that moment . . . " What? Sign, line, fine, shine? Nothing served as well as the unwanted "divine." I never could find a way out. The song written in 1937 shows signs of being a long-lived

28

standard ballad—but I shall never be happy with that word!

The word "dream" is a much overworked word, and yet it seems almost impossible to do without because it means so many things—all of them beautiful. It is un-specifically pleasant and lovely. When I started to write my most recent set of lyrics, those for *South Pacific*, I made up my mind not to use it at all. Now that I look over the score, I find it appearing more often than in any score I have ever written.

I had a strange experience with this word in connection with a song I wrote for a picture back in 1935. I was collaborating with Sigmund Romberg. He wrote a beauti-ful, simple waltz. I fell in love with it. I was certain that everybody would, if I could match the even simplicity of the melody with words of the same quality. The refrain lyrically consists of eight lines. It took me three weeks to write them. One of the lines is repeated twice, so that what I wrote came to only six lines. I had a terrific tussle with this song. The first or second day I was working on it, the music suggested the title, "When I Grow Too Old to Dream." I was delighted with it when I first thought of it. It was so easy to sing. It was so smooth. It was so much in mood with the music. The music was born for it. The next line came very naturally. I sang to myself: "When I grow too old to dream, I'll have you to remember." This was going to be easy to write. I would knock this off in an hour or two. Then I stopped suddenly. What did it mean? "When I grow too old to dream"—

when are you too old to dream? Too old for what kind of dreams? As a matter of fact, when you are old, aren't you likely to dream more than at any other time in your life? Don't you look back and dream about the past? How did this silly line ever come into my head? I threw it aside and worked on another title, then another and another. I finished several refrains based on other titles. I didn't like any of them. In the intervals between each of these efforts, I would go back to the title, "When I Grow Too Old to Dream," and try to convince myself that it did mean something. Then I would reject it again, but regretfully, because it had some quality which appealed to me as a songwriter, and I loved to sing it to myself alone in my study. It became so insistent that I began to wonder whether my instinct wasn't truer than my reason. If this line didn't mean anything, why was it so attractive to me? I reanalyzed it and asked myself why my brain had created it, and why I had loved it as soon as I had invented it. I concluded that I must be giving the word "dream" a special meaning, that I was thinking of it in the sense of a lover dreaming only about the present and the future. In saying "When I grow too old to dream," I was really saying, "When I grow too old to love you and to dream about loving you, I'll have you to remember, I will be remembering our love in the past."

> "When I grow too old to dream,
> I'll have you to remember,
> When I grow too old to dream,
> Your love will live in my heart."

I knew what I meant by this, but I was by no means sure that my special conception of the word "dream" would get over to other people. It was a song of farewell, the rest of the refrain being:

> "So kiss me, my sweet,
> And so let us part,
> And when I grow too old to dream,
> Your kiss will live in my heart."

Well, I liked it. In fact, I adored it, and I walked up and down my study, singing it to myself and feeling that if I liked it so well perhaps other people would too and would not be too intellectually analytical. I submitted it to the composer and he was delighted. So were the producer and the director of the picture and the gentlemen who were working on the screenplay. My publisher too thought it was a great song, and I kept my mouth shut and didn't even suggest to any of them that I was in doubt about its semantic correctness.

The picture was released, and was a spectacular failure. The song, however, became a solid success. The man who published it talked to me about it months later, and asked me exactly what it meant. I said, "I'm not quite sure," and he laughed very loudly. He'd apparently talked it over with some other songwriters and they had all wondered about it. The important point in this story is that while this lyric is academically unjustifiable, there is something about it that caught me and caught the public in exactly the same way, and the only way I can explain it is that this special conception of the word "dream" got through to them. They accepted the word as meaning "dream in the future," or "have youthful dreams." I am sure that the music has a great deal to do with the acceptance of these words. Hearing the melody with them, the listener is mesmerized and lulled emotionally. The words, instead of being literal, are like music superimposed on music. The lyric and the melody swing together in a happy union, and the pleasure they find in each other infects the singer and the listener with a kind of irresponsible satisfaction. Gertrude Stein has, of course, this unspecific approach to the use of words, and Edith Sitwell in her group of songs entitled *Façade* has made a deliberate attempt to write words with special emphasis on sound and very little attention to meaning or clarity. I do not believe that the future of good lyric writing lies in this direction, but my experience with "When I Grow Too Old to Dream" forces me to admit that there is something in the idea. It belongs with the general flight from literalism in all art expression—notably painting—which characterizes the creative works of this century. In an age commonly called scientific, we are steadily becoming more and more indefinite and mystic. This, however, is a subject for another book or many books by authors more scientific or mystic than I.

Rhyming, phonetics, semantics—all very important. But technique and professional polish do not make a song. They improve it and their absence might ruin it, but there is an element much less tangible that is the deciding factor in a song's life. One evening this summer I was on Arthur Godfrey's television program. He told me that he was continually besieged by young songwriters. He said that almost everyone seemed to have written his one song and wanted to find out how to get it before the public. I told Arthur that I'd had an entirely different experience. Most young songwriters or amateur songwriters of all ages who have approached me have told me that they had at least forty songs—sometimes four hundred songs. Most of them make the point that they can rattle them off very quickly, one a day or as many as anyone would wish. "Songs just come to me," many people tell me. If I met a man with just one song, I would be more interested in him. I believe that anyone who stated sincerely what was deep in his heart could not only write a song, but could quickly get it published because it would be sure to be a good song. What actually happens in the case of practically all amateur writers is that they are imitating other men's songs. They are being, or trying to be, Irving Berlin or Cole Porter, or they are trying to imitate some of the songs currently on The Hit Parade. My observation about amateurs is that they are money-mad. The professional loves songs and loves songwriting. The amateurs want some quick money and think that songwriting is an easy way to get it. They want to believe that the main trick is to get to know some publisher, or a bandleader, or someone who will exploit their manuscript. But they don't spend enough time on each manuscript. They submit songs in their first draft. They don't go over them painstakingly as professional writers do, and they don't in the first instance dig it up out of their own brains and hearts.

The most important ingredient of a good song is sincerity. Let the song be yours and yours alone. However important, however trivial, believe it. Mean it from the bottom of your heart, and say what is on your mind as carefully, as clearly, as beautifully as you can. Show it to no one until you are certain that you cannot make one change that would improve it. After that, however, be willing to make improvements if someone can convince you that they are needed.

This sounds like simple advice, but no one knows better than I how hard it is to follow. The basic rules are always the hardest ones to observe, even though they seem the easiest. No beginner on the golf course or the tennis courts questions the good sense of his first lesson when he is told to keep his eye on the ball. This seems such an obvious thing to do, and yet no matter how many years you play these games your chief mistake remains taking your eye off the ball. This tendency to skip over the fundamental things and grasp the superficial is the tragedy of man's history from the beginning of time. I do not, therefore, place undue blame on misguided songwriters. They are merely keeping up the tradition of the stupidity of the human race when, instead of writing what they honestly feel, they invent fancy rhymes and foolish jokes and tricky titles and imitative phrases and lines that merely "fill in." I do not blame them if they spend their days trying to get to know someone who knows someone who is the brother-in-law of a publisher. I am just saying that all these things are a waste of time without a good manuscript. Get the right words and the right notes down on paper and, in some way, your song will reach the public. Publishers are looking for good songs. They often make mistakes and reject good ones and accept bad ones, but I do not believe that all the publishers will ever reject a really good song. Somebody will appreciate its quality. If a publisher doesn't, some record company will. The people who claim that the publishing and songwriting game is a tight ring into which beginners are not permitted are usually people with carelessly written manuscripts in their briefcases. The men who write the good songs haven't time for all this kind of talk. They are too busy writing and loving what they write before they show it to anybody else.

If I seem unfairly severe on the amateur songwriter, the source of my intolerance is my own history. When I first began writing, I too made all these same mistakes, and I am frantically anxious to prevent others from making them. I used to write songs very quickly. A Long Island commuter, I prided myself that I could often write a refrain on one trip into New York, and the verse on the way back that night. Not many of these were good songs. I was too easily satisfied with my work. I was too often trying to emulate older and better lyric writers, saying things similar to the things they were saying. It

35

would have been all right had I been content to imitate the forms of their songs, but the substance should have been mine and it was not. I know that insincerity held me back for several years, and I know that even after I'd had a period of success, it again handicapped me and caused me to have failures. Loathing all dishonest and sloppy work for the sorrows it has caused me, I loathe it in others as I would any poison, and if I can knock it out of anyone, I will.

When successful men discuss their careers, they are prone to leave out some of their early mistakes and humiliating failures. This is true not only of autobiographical after-dinner speeches, but also of most biographies and profiles of prominent people. There is a desire to create the illusion of a magic touch and infallibility, and I think this does a great deal of harm. In the early days of his own career the novice is, of course, making mistakes. If he is told that somebody else got to the top making no mistakes at all, he is likely to doubt his own talents. He compares his gawky rawness with what seems to have been the perfection of the successful man as a youth, and he says to himself: "If successful men were like that when they were my age, how will I ever catch up to them?"

Everyone is kicked around during his apprentice years, and in his fear and ignorance he makes silly blunders and does silly things of which he is ashamed later. If every successful man were to confess these past errors, he could do a great service to those young people who are trying to follow in his footsteps. The legend of George Washington's abnormal juvenile honesty has discouraged many children who, knowing that they have told lies, believe that they are marked for life and can never attain importance or even respect in their communities. These apparently irrelevant observations constitute a prelude to some confessions and disclosures I believe I should make about my own seamy past. I intend to quote some of my early efforts, the main motive being to reassure younger writers. Knowing how bad I was at one time, I hope that they will be encouraged.

Consider a little number that wowed them in the Columbia University Varsity Show of 1917. The show was called *Home, James*. The composer of the score was Robert Lippmann, who is now one of New York City's most successful and prominent orthopedists. To be perfectly fair to myself, I cannot take the entire blame for the lyric because it was written in collaboration with Herman Axelrod, a friend of mine in a class above me, who later turned to real estate.

Here is our lyric:

ANNIE McGINNIS PAVLOVA

Clancey was fond of a show,
From opera to movies he'd go.
On dancin' and prancin' Clancey was keen,
But the Ballet Russe he never had seen.
For five dollars a throw he decided to go
And he bought him a seat in the very first row.
Annie came out. Clancey yelled, "Stop her!
She ain't no Roosian, for I knew her poppa."

37

Annie McGinnis Pavlova,
I'll stop you from puttin' one over,
'Twas in Hogan's back alley,
You learned the bacchanale
And now you're the pride of the Ballet Russe.
They call you a zephyr, a fairy, an elf,
Put on your flannels, take care of yourself!
For the costume you're wearin's a shame to old Erin,
Oh Annie, you'd better go home.

There was another little ditty in *Home, James,* the
first two lines of which were:

"I want to be a star in moving pictures,
Like Chaplin, Pickford, Fairbanks and the other
fixtures."

Quite a rhyme! Like my two collaborators, I expected
to make my living in another calling. I was studying law,
but before I finished my course I called upon my uncle,
who was a theatrical producer, and asked him for a job.
He made me an assistant stage manager. He knew that I
wished to become a writer, but he very wisely admonished
me not to write for at least a year, during which time I
could acquire some practical backstage experience. Within
the year he produced a play by another author who, being
pressed for time, permitted me to write part of the opening chorus. This was my first professional work. I was
writing a lyric for a hostess to greet her guests shortly
after the curtain rose. What I remember of the lyric goes
like this:

"Make yourselves at home,
'Neath our spacious dome.
Do just as you please
In twos or threes, if you'd rather—
But rest assured you'll be no bother."

How did she know they would be no bother? As I remember a bizarre assemblage coming on the stage, carrying tennis rackets, wearing riding clothes and sport costumes of outrageous color, it seemed almost certain that they would raise hell with her house before the week-end was over.

Later in my career, after I had had three or four shows produced on Broadway, I remember writing a lyric called "My Little Redskin" which was a real horror. The female chorus came out with a deep sunburned make-up and wearing bathing suits, and the lyric featured the double meaning of "redskin"—the term applied to American Indians and the literal description of their sunburn. Get it? I don't remember this lyric. I could find it somewhere because it was published, but I am not going to look for it. There are limits to which I will debase myself, even to encourage the young.

During the early twenties, when I was making my start, I don't believe that musical comedy standards were as high as they are today. We followed a rigid construction formula. There was always an opening chorus at the rise of the curtain, and it was never expected that the audience would understand the words. The girls and boys were picked for all-around work, singing, dancing

and appearance. The appearance was the first consideration. Most of them were indifferent singers and the
quality of their dancing was due more to the agility and
energy of their youth than to their training. As a matter
of fact, when I was a stage manager, I used to train the
understudies and the replacements for all the dancers.
There was no step that they did that I couldn't do or, at
any rate, show them how to do.

After the opening chorus came a number professionally
called the "icebreaker." This was admittedly not one of
the major efforts of the composer and lyric writer. It was
a fill-in song written to quiet down the audience after
the opening chorus and postpone any important action
in the story until all the latecomers had been seated. In
other words, if you got to the theater on time you had to
sit through several minutes of nothing at all, waiting for
those who chose to come late. Today they still come late,
but we don't wait for them. We start our play when the
curtain rises. A much better idea, I think. The very existence of the "icebreaker" indicates a lack of integrity in
the musical comedy writing of those days. The composer
and lyric writer concentrated mainly on a few major
efforts: a big dance number, a love ballad, a light comedy
duet and one or two songs for the comedians (in the
latter, while the author would try to write the best jokes
he could, the composer would write music which was not
out of his top drawer—he did not want to waste a good
melody on a comedy song). I'm speaking, of course, of a
general attitude. It would not be true of earlier craftsmen

40

like Gilbert and Sullivan. In no period have the really fine musical plays been tainted by this shoddy approach. *The Merry Widow* is a galaxy of wonderful songs. Victor Herbert's *The Red Mill* is another example of a score marred by no "fill-ins." The general attitude, however, toward musical comedy was cynical. Neither the public nor the critics expected more than a display of girls, jokes and tunes. Those who came off with the most credit in addition to the stars were several prominent producers (Florenz Ziegfeld, Charles Dillingham, Arthur Hammerstein) and composers (Jerome Kern, Lou Hirsch, George Gershwin, Richard Rodgers, Vincent Youmans, Sigmund Romberg, Rudolf Friml). The librettist was a kind of stable boy. If the race was won he was seldom mentioned. If the race was lost he was blamed for giving the horse the wrong feed. For many years I read theatrical criticism and comment which contained the statement "The book of a musical show doesn't matter," and yet in the case of most failures it was pointed out that the book was so bad that it could not be survived.

This attitude was not conducive to an author's self-respect. The field of libretto writing therefore was filled with hacks and gag men who extended the tradition of ignominy attached to musical comedy books. There were, on the other hand, a few patient authors who kept on writing well-constructed musical plays, most of which were successful, and they continued to give their best with very little chance of being praised for their efforts. Among these was my dear friend and erstwhile tutor,

Otto Harbach. Over a long period of years, he was the author or co-author of such musical successes as *The Three Twins, Madam Sherry, The Firefly, Wildflower, Mary, Rose Marie, No, No, Nanette, Whoopee, Sunny, The Desert Song, The Cat and the Fiddle,* and *Roberta.* These plays were written with many composers: Hoschner, Friml, Kern, Hirsch, Romberg, Youmans.

It is almost unbelievable that a man with this record of achievement received so little recognition. I feel this, perhaps, more than anyone because I know so well his unusual attainments as an artist, and because I am so indebted to him. I was born into the theatrical world with two gold spoons in my mouth. One was my uncle, Arthur Hammerstein, who took me into his producing organization after I left law school and gave me wise guidance. It was he, too, who supplied the second gold spoon, Otto Harbach. Otto Harbach, at my uncle's persuasion, accepted me as a collaborator. It is true that this was not entirely a gesture of friendship on Otto's part. I know that he thought well of my talents at the time and saw promise in me. From the very start, our relationship was that of two collaborators on an equal footing, although he was twenty years older than I and had written many successes while I had been going to school and college. His generosity in dividing credits and royalties equally with me was the least of his favors. Much more important were the things he taught me about writing for the theater. Otto is the best play analyst I have ever met. He is also a patient man and a born teacher. Like most young writers, I had a great eagerness to get words down on paper. He taught me to think a long time before actually writing. He taught me most of the precepts I have already stated in these notes. He taught me never to stop work on anything if you can think of one small improvement to make. To speak of his nonprofessional qualities as a civilized human being is completely irrelevant to these notes. Please, nevertheless, let me record that he is the kindest, most tolerant and wisest man I have ever met.

There are some people in the theater who have helped me so much that it is difficult to imagine where I would be, or what I would be, if I had not met them. There was Herbert Stothart, the first composer with whom I collaborated professionally. He was a conductor for my uncle's musical productions, and I was the stage manager. During the actors' strike we had an enforced idleness on which we capitalized by writing a musical play together. It was he who sold it to my uncle because, while I was reading it, Herb burst into such uncontrollable laughter every time I read a line purporting to be funny, that my uncle thought he was listening to the most comic script ever written.

Most of my collaborators were older than I, seven, ten or twenty years older. I benefited by their experience. They constituted a series of short-cuts for me, guiding me off rocky roads that I would have traveled had I been going alone. Jerome Kern boosted me several rungs up the ladder when he invited me to write *Show Boat* with him after he'd acquired the rights from Edna Ferber. During my several collaborations with Jerry I absorbed his habit of being painstaking about very small things. I was surprised at first to find him deeply concerned about details which I thought did not matter much when there were so many important problems to solve in connection with writing and producing a play. He proved to me, eventually, that while people may not take any particular notice of any one small effect, the over-all result of finickiness like his produces a polish which an audience appreciates. Beyond my professional profit from working with Jerry, I enjoyed one of the warmest and most stimulating friendships with which I have been blessed.

Sigmund Romberg got me into the habit of working hard. In our first collaboration, *The Desert Song,* I used to visit him in an apartment which he had in the Hotel Marie Antoinette in the Sixties on Broadway. I remember one day bringing up a finished lyric to him. He played it over and said, "It fits." Then he turned to me and asked me, "What else have you got?" I said that I didn't have anything more, but I would go away and set another melody. He persuaded me to stay right there and write it while he was working on something else. He put me in another room with a pad and a pencil. Afraid to come out empty-handed, I finished another refrain that afternoon.

I have written many plays and pictures with "Rommy" and his highest praise has been always the same, "It fits." Disappointed at first at such limited approval, I learned later that what he meant was not merely that the words fitted the notes, but that they matched the spirit of his music and that he thought they were fine.

When I wrote the opening chorus of our first joint effort, *The Desert Song*—very likely closed up in that room at the Marie Antoinette—I was not very careful about the lyric. I knew that it was to be sung by a male chorus, and they would bellow it very loudly and indistinguishably. I wrote words that could be sung out comfortably without any particular attention to shaded meanings. It turned out as I had anticipated. It was an effective opening from a musical standpoint, and nobody knew what the words were, and I didn't care. A year after the American première I went to London to assist in the production there. Then, to my dismay, I heard the English male chorus singing. They were clipping their consonants so sharply that every word could be understood! I felt like a cornered criminal. It was a lesson to me. Thereafter, I assumed always that someday, somebody might sing even an opening chorus so that it could be understood and, therefore, the words had better be good.

This is a very important thing for writers to remember. You never know when you will be found out if your work is careless. A year or so ago, on the cover of the New York *Herald Tribune* Sunday Magazine, I saw a picture of the Statue of Liberty. It was a picture taken from a helicopter and it showed the top of the statue's head. I was amazed at the detail there. The sculptor had

45

done a painstaking job with the lady's coiffure, and yet he must have been pretty sure that the only eyes that would ever see this detail would be the uncritical eyes of sea gulls. He could not have dreamt that any man would ever fly over this head and take a picture of it. He was artist enough, however, to finish off this part of the statue with as much care as he had devoted to her face and her arms and the torch and everything that people can see as they sail up the bay. He was right. When you are creating a work of art, or any other kind of work, finish the job off perfectly. You never know when a helicopter, or some other instrument not at the moment invented, may come along and find you out.

I have mentioned the fact that most of my collaborators were older than I. Richard Rodgers, with whom I am now collaborating, is seven years younger. This is the first time I have had an agreement with a composer contemplating exclusive collaboration with him. In the past I have worked with many men, shifting from one to the other according to the project of the moment. Dick, on the other hand, up until the time he started to write with me, had only one partner, Lorenz Hart. There are advantages to this kind of collaboration, provided that the two people get along as well as we do. We have fallen into a rhythm of work which suits us both. Our social lives and our personal habits are similar. Our theatrical tastes and standards are as nearly identical as they could be. The course of our professional union has been incredibly smooth and happy.

Collaboration is the biggest word in the theater. It is the most important element in theatrical success. Not just the collaboration between an author and a composer, but the total collaboration in every play, the convergence and co-ordination of all the different talents, producing, writing, directing, choreography, acting, scene designing, costume designing, lighting, orchestration, theater management, company management, public relations — the mixture of all these ingredients is essential to every theatrical meal that seeks to make itself palatable to the public. To get along in the theater you must enjoy working side by side with other people. You must be willing not only to give your best to them but to accept their best and give them the opportunity of adding their efforts to yours to their full capacities.

One novelist recently stated that she was leaving the theater and returning to writing exclusively for the printed page. She said that she could not stand so many people advising her and helping her and butting in on her work. She did not like the feel of the director's hot breath on her neck. She was right to leave. If you want privacy in your work, and if you want to make your flights of fancy solo, stay away from the theater. The theater is a welding of many arts into one. No one person can be efficient or talented in all these arts, and if any man could write and produce and direct and act and play the music, shift the scenery, design the costumes and, in short, do everything that could be done on one stage and come up with what was literally a one-man show, he would still need one more thing, an audience. You cannot get away from collaboration.

I am discontented with what I have written here. I have not said nearly all I would like to say about lyrics and the plays for which I write them. "I could go on and on" but I don't dare. I feel the self-consciousness of a man who is madly in love with a girl and wants to talk about her but has already imposed too long on his friends' time and politeness. If I have been long-winded, please forgive me my extravagances and indulge my blind infatuation. I'm in love with a wonderful theater.

from OKLAHOMA!

MUSIC BY RICHARD RODGERS

OH, WHAT A
BEAUTIFUL MORNIN'!

There's a bright, golden haze on the meadow,
There's a bright, golden haze on the meadow.
The corn is as high as a elephant's eye,
An' it looks like it's climbin' clear up to the sky.

Oh, what a beautiful mornin'!
Oh, what a beautiful day!
I got a beautiful feelin'
Ev'rythin's goin' my way.

All the cattle are standin' like statues,
All the cattle are standin' like statues.
They don't turn their heads as they see me ride by,
But a little brown mav'rick is winkin' her eye.

Oh, what a beautiful mornin'!
Oh, what a beautiful day!
I got a beautiful feelin'
Ev'rythin's goin' my way.

All the sounds of the earth are like music—
All the sounds of the earth are like music.
The breeze is so busy it don't miss a tree,
And a ol' weepin' willer is laughin' at me.

Oh, what a beautiful mornin'!
Oh, what a beautiful day!
I got a beautiful feelin'
Ev'rythin's goin' my way . . .
Oh, what a beautiful day!

THE SURREY WITH THE
FRINGE ON TOP

When I take you out tonight with me,
Honey, here's the way it's goin' to be:
You will set behind a team of snow-white horses
In the slickest gig you ever see!

Chicks and ducks and geese better scurry
When I take you out in the surrey,
When I take you out in the surrey with the fringe on top.
Watch thet fringe and see how it flutters
When I drive them high-steppin' strutters—
Nosey-pokes'll peek through their shutters and their eyes
        will pop!
The wheels are yeller, the upholstery's brown,
The dashboard's genuine leather,
With isinglass curtains y' c'n roll right down
In case there's a change in the weather;
Two bright side lights winkin' and blinkin',
Ain't no finer rig, I'm a-thinkin';
You c'n keep yer rig if you're thinkin' 'at I'd keer to swap
Fer that shiny little surrey with the fringe on the top.

Would y' say the fringe was made of silk?
Wouldn't have no other kind but silk.
Has it really got a team of snow-white horses?
One's like snow—the other's more like milk.

All the world'll fly in a flurry
When I take you out in the surrey,
When I take you out in the surrey with the fringe on top.
When we hit that road, hell fer leather,
Cats and dogs'll dance in the heather,
Birds and frogs'll sing all together, and the toads will hop!
The wind'll whistle as we rattle along,
The cows'll moo in the clover,
The river will ripple out a whispered song,
And whisper it over and over:
Don't you wisht y'd go on ferever?
Don't you wisht y'd go on ferever?
Don't you wisht y'd go on ferever and ud never stop
In that shiny little surrey with the fringe on the top?

I can see the stars gittin' blurry
When we ride back home in the surrey,
Ridin' slowly home in the surrey with the fringe on top.
I can feel the day gittin' older,
Feel a sleepy head near my shoulder,
Noddin', droopin' close to my shoulder till it falls, kerplop!
The sun is swimmin' on the rim of a hill,

The moon is takin' a header,
And jist as I'm thinkin' all the earth is still,
A lark'll wake up in the medder . . .
Hush! You bird, my baby's a-sleepin'—
Maybe got a dream worth a-keepin'.
Whoa! You team, and jist keep a-creepin' at a slow
       clip-clop;
Don't you hurry with the surrey with the fringe on the
       top.

KANSAS CITY

I got to Kansas City on a Frid'y.
By Sattidy I l'arned a thing or two.
For up to then I didn't have an idy
Of whut the modren world was comin' to.
I counted twenty gas buggies goin' by theirsel's
Almost ev'ry time I tuck a walk.
Nen I put my ear to a Bell Telephone,
And a strange womern started in to talk!

Ev'rythin's up to date in Kansas City.
They've gone about as fur as they c'n go!
They went and built a skyscraper seven stories high—
About as high as a buildin' orta grow.
Ev'rythin's like a dream in Kansas City.
It's better than a magic-lantern show.
Y' c'n turn the radiator on whenever you want some heat,
With ev'ry kind o' comfort ev'ry house is all complete,
You c'n walk to privies in the rain an' never wet yer feet—
They've gone about as fur as they c'n go!
Yes, sir!
They've gone about as fur as they c'n go!

Ev'rythin's up to date in Kansas City.
They've gone about as fur as they c'n go!
They got a big theayter they call a burleekew.
Fer fifty cents you c'n see a dandy show.
One of the gals was fat and pink and pretty,
As round above as she was round below.
I could swear that she was padded from her shoulder to
       her heel,
But later in the second act, when she began to peel,
She proved that ev'rythin' she had was absolutely real—
She went about as fur as she could go!
Yes, sir!
She went about as fur as she could go!

I CAIN'T SAY NO

It ain't so much a question of not knowin' whut to do,
I knowed whut's right and wrong since I been ten.
I heared a lot of stories—and I reckon they are true—
About how girls're put upon by men.
I know I mustn't fall into the pit,
But when I'm with a feller—I fergit!

I'm jist a girl who cain't say no,
I'm in a turrible fix.
I always say, "Come on, le's go!"
Jist when I orta say nix!
When a person tries to kiss a girl
I know she orta give his face a smack.
But as soon as someone kisses me
I somehow sorta wanta kiss him back.
I'm jist a fool when lights are low.
I cain't be prissy and quaint—
I ain't the type thet c'n faint—
How c'n I be whut I ain't?
I cain't say no!

Whut you goin' to do when a feller gits flirty
And starts to talk purty?
Whut you goin' to do?

58

S'posin' 'at he says 'at yer lips're like cherries,
Er roses, er berries?
Whut you goin' to do?
S'posin' 'at he says 'at you're sweeter'n cream
And he's gotta have cream er die?
Whut you goin' to do when he talks thet way?
Spit in his eye?

I'm jist a girl who cain't say no,
Cain't seem to say it at all.
I hate to disserpoint a beau
When he is payin' a call.
Fer a while I ack refined and cool,
A-settin' on the velveteen settee—
Nen I think of thet ol' golden rule,
And do fer him whut he would do fer me.
I cain't resist a Romeo
In a sombrero and chaps.
Soon as I sit on their laps
Somethin' inside of me snaps—
I cain't say no!

I'm jist a girl who cain't say no.
Kissin's my favorite food.
With er without the mistletoe
I'm in a holiday mood.
Other girls are coy and hard to catch,
But other girls ain't havin' any fun.

59

Ev'ry time I lose a wrestlin' match
I have a funny feelin' that I won.
Though I c'n feel the undertow,
I never make a complaint
Till it's too late fer restraint,
Then when I want to I cain't—
I cain't say no!

MANY A NEW DAY

Why should a womern who is healthy and strong
Blubber like a baby if her man goes away?
A-weepin' and a-wailin' how he's done her wrong—
That's one thing you'll never hear me say!
Never gonna think that the man I lose
Is the only man among men.
I'll snap my fingers to show I don't care.
I'll buy me a brand-new dress to wear.
I'll scrub my neck and I'll bresh my hair,
And start all over again!

Many a new face will please my eye,
Many a new love will find me.
Never've I once looked back to sigh
Over the romance behind me.
Many a new day will dawn before I do!
Many a light lad may kiss and fly,
A kiss gone by is bygone;
Never've I asked an August sky,
"Where has last July gone?"
Never've I wandered through the rye,
Wonderin' where has some guy gone—
Many a new day will dawn before I do!

Many a new face will please my eye,
Many a new love will find me.
Never've I once looked back to sigh
Over the romance behind me.
Many a new day will dawn before I do!
Never've I chased the honeybee
Who carelessly cajoled me;
Somebody else just as sweet as he
Cheered me and consoled me.
Never've I wept into my tea
Over the deal someone doled me—
Many a new day will dawn,
Many a red sun will set,
Many a blue moon will shine, before I do!

PEOPLE WILL SAY
WE'RE IN LOVE

Don't throw bouquets at me,
Don't please my folks too much,
Don't laugh at my jokes too much—
People will say we're in love!
Don't sigh and gaze at me
(Your sighs are so like mine),
Your eyes mustn't glow like mine—
People will say we're in love!
Don't start collecting things
(Give me my rose and my glove);
Sweetheart, they're suspecting things—
People will say we're in love!

Don't praise my charm too much,
Don't look so vain with me,
Don't stand in the rain with me—
People will say we're in love!
Don't take my arm too much,
Don't keep your hand in mine.
Your hand looks so grand in mine,
People will say we're in love!
Don't dance all night with me,
Till the stars fade from above.
They'll see it's all right with me,
People will say we're in love!

PORE JUD IS DAID

(*JUD is a "bullet-colored, growly man" who lives alone in a smokehouse, nursing his neuroses. A cowhand, CURLY, has just shocked and infuriated him by suggesting that he hang himself. Now, however, he has excited Jud's curiosity in what the funeral would be like.*)

JUD
Would they be any flowers, d'you think?

CURLY
Shore would, and palms, too,
All around yer cawfin. Nen folks ud stand around
   you,
And the men ud bare their heads,
And the womern ud sniffle softly.
Some'd prob'ly faint—
Ones that had tuck a shine to you
When you wuz alive.

JUD
Whut womern have tuck a shine to me?

CURLY
Lots of womern. On'y they don't never come right out and show you how they feel less'n you die first.

64

JUD
(Thoughtfully)
I guess that's so.

CURLY
They'd shore sing loud though when the singin' started—
sing like their hearts ud break!

> Pore Jud is daid,
> Pore Jud Fry is daid,
> All gether round his cawfin now and cry.
> He had a heart of gold
> And he wasn't very old—
> Oh, why did sich a feller have to die?
> Pore Jud is daid,
> Pore Jud Fry is daid,
> He's lookin', oh, so peaceful and serene—

JUD
(Touched and suddenly carried away)
And serene!

CURLY
He's all laid out to rest
With his hands acrost his chest.
His fingernails have never b'en so clean.

(JUD *turns slowly to question the good taste of this last reference, but* CURLY *plunges straight into another item of the imagined wake.*)

65

Nen the preacher'd git up and he'd say:

"Folks! We are gethered here to moan and groan over
    our brother Jud Fry,

Who hung hisse'f up by a rope in the smokehouse."

Nen there'd be weepin' and wailin' from some of those
    womern.

Nen he'd say, "Jud was the most misunderstood man in
    the territory.

People useter think he was a mean, ugly feller,

And they called him a dirty skunk and a ornery pig-
    stealer.

But the folks 'at really knowed him,

Knowed 'at beneath them two dirty shirts he alw'ys wore,

There beat a heart as big as all outdoors."

JUD

As big as all outdoors.

CURLY

Jud Fry loved his fellow man.

JUD

He loved his fellow man.

CURLY
(*Speaking with the impassioned inflections of an evangelist*)

He loved the birds of the forest and the beasts of the field.

He loved the mice and the vermin in the barn,

And he treated the rats like equals—which was right.

And he loved little children.

66

He loved ev'body and ev'thin' in the world . . .
On'y he never let on, so nobody ever knowed it!

> Pore Jud is daid,
> Pore Jud Fry is daid,
> His friends'll weep and wail fer miles around.

JUD

Miles around.

CURLY

> The daisies in the dell
> Will give out a diff'runt smell
> Becuz pore Jud is underneath the ground.

> (JUD *is too emotionally exalted by the spirit of*
> CURLY'S *singing to be analytical. He now*
> *takes up a refrain of his own.*)

JUD

> Pore Jud is daid,
> A candle lights his haid,
> He's layin' in a cawfin made of wood.

CURLY

Wood.

JUD

> And folks are feelin' sad
> Cuz they useter treat him bad,
> And now they know their friend has gone fer
>   good.

67

CURLY
(*Softly*)
Good.

JUD AND CURLY
Pore Jud is daid,
A candle lights his haid—

CURLY
He's lookin', oh, so purty and so nice!
He looks like he's asleep.
It's a shame that he won't keep,
But it's summer and we're runnin' out of ice . . .
Pore Jud—pore Jud!

(JUD *breaks down, weeps, and sits at the table,
burying his head in his arms.*)

Yes, sir. That's the way it ud be. Shore be a interestin'
    funril.
Wouldn't like to miss it.

68

LONELY ROOM

The floor creaks,
The door squeaks,
There's a field mouse a-nibblin' on a broom,
And I set by myself
Like a cobweb on a shelf,
By myself in a lonely room.

But when there's a moon in my winder
And it slants down a beam 'crost my bed,
Then the shadder of a tree starts a-dancin' on the
    wall
And a dream starts a-dancin' in my head.
And all the things that I wish fer
Turn out like I want them to be,
And I'm better'n that smart-aleck cowhand
Who thinks he is better'n me,
And the girl that I want
Ain't afraid of my arms,
And her own soft arms keep me warm.
And her long, yeller hair
Falls acrost my face
Jist like the rain in a storm . . .

The floor creaks,
The door squeaks,

And the mouse starts a-nibblin' on the broom.
And the sun flicks my eyes—
It was all a pack o' lies!
I'm awake in a lonely room.

OUT OF MY DREAMS

Out of my dreams and into your arms I long to fly.
I will come as evening comes to woo a waiting sky.
Out of my dreams and into the hush of falling shadows,
When the mist is low, and stars are breaking through,
Then out of my dreams I'll go,
Into a dream with you.

OKLAHOMA!

They couldn't pick a better time to start in life,
It ain't too early and it ain't too late.
Startin' as a farmer with a brand-new wife—
Soon be livin' in a brand-new state!
Brand-new state
Gonna treat you great!

> Gonna give you barley,
> Carrots and pertaters—
> Pasture fer the cattle—
> Spinach and termayters!
> Flowers on the prairie where the June bugs
>   zoom—
> Plen'y of air and plen'y of room—
> Plen'y of room to swing a rope,
> Plen'y of heart and plen'y of hope.

Oklahoma,
Where the wind comes sweepin' down the plain
(And the wavin' wheat
Can sure smell sweet
When the wind comes right behind the rain)
Oklahoma!
Every night my honey lamb and I
Sit alone and talk

And watch a hawk
Makin' lazy circles in the sky.
We know we belong to the land,
And the land we belong to is grand.
And when we say:
Ee-ee-ow! A-yip-i-o-ee-ay!
We're only sayin',
You're doin' fine, Oklahoma!
Oklahoma, O.K.!

from STATE FAIR

MUSIC BY RICHARD RODGERS

IT MIGHT AS WELL
BE SPRING

I'm as restless as a willow in a windstorm,
I'm as jumpy as a puppet on a string!
(I'd say that I had spring fever,
But I know it isn't spring.)
I am starry-eyed and vaguely discontented,
Like a nightingale without a song to sing.
(Oh, why should I have spring fever
When it isn't even spring?)

I keep wishing I were somewhere else,
Walking down a strange new street,
Hearing words that I have never heard
From a man I've yet to meet.

I'm as busy as a spider, spinning daydreams,
I'm as giddy as a baby on a swing.
I haven't seen a crocus or a rosebud
Or a robin on the wing,
But I feel so gay—in a melancholy way—
That it might as well be spring . . .
It might as well be spring.

THAT'S FOR ME

I saw you standing in the sun,
And you were something to see.
I know what I like, and I liked what I saw,
And I said to myself,
"That's for me!"

"A lovely morning," I remarked,
And you were quick to agree.
You wanted to walk and I nodded my head
As I breathlessly said,
"That's for me."

I left you standing under stars—
The day's adventures are through.
There's nothing for me but the dream in my heart,
And the dream in my heart—
That's for you,
      Oh, my darling,
      That's for you!

IT'S A GRAND NIGHT
FOR SINGING

It's a grand night for singing,
The moon is flying high,
And somewhere a bird who is bound he'll be heard,
Is throwing his heart at the sky.
It's a grand night for singing,
The stars are bright above,
The earth is aglow, and, to add to the show,
I think I am falling in love,
Falling, falling in love.

from CAROUSEL

MUSIC BY RICHARD RODGERS

JUNE IS BUSTIN' OUT
ALL OVER

March went out like a lion,
A-whippin' up the water in the bay.
Then April cried
And stepped aside,
And along come pretty little May!

May was full of promises,
But she didn't keep 'em quick enough fer some,
And a crowd of Doubtin' Thomases
Was predictin' that the summer'd never come.

But it's comin, by gum!
Y' ken feel it come,
Y' ken feel it in yer heart,
Y' ken see it in the ground,
Y' ken hear it in the trees,
Y' ken smell it in the breeze—
Look around, look around, look around!

June is bustin' out all over!
All over the meadow and the hill,
Buds're bustin' outa bushes,
And the rompin' river pushes
Ev'ry little wheel that wheels beside a mill.

83

June is bustin' out all over!
The feelin' is gettin' so intense
That the young Virginia creepers
Hev been huggin' the bejeepers
Outa all the mornin'-glories on the fence.
Because it's June!
June, June, June—
Jest because it's June—June—June!

Fresh and alive and gay and young,
June is a love song sweetly sung.

June is bustin' out all over!
The saplin's are bustin' out with sap!
Love hes found my brother, "Junior,"
And my sister's even lunier,
And my ma is gettin' kittenish with Pap.
June is bustin' out all over!
To ladies the men are payin' court.
Lotsa ships are kept at anchor
Jest because the captains hanker
Fer a comfort they ken only get in port!
Because it's June!
June, June, June—
Jest because it's June—June—June!

June makes the bay look bright and new,
Sails gleamin' white on sunlit blue.

84

June is bustin' out all over!
The ocean is full of Jacks and Jills.
With her little tail a-swishin'
Ev'ry lady fish is wishin'
That a male would come and grab her by the gills!
June is bustin' out all over!
The sheep aren't sleepin' any more.
All the rams that chase the ewe sheep
Are determined there'll be new sheep,
And the ewe sheep aren't even keepin' score!
On accounta it's June!
June, June, June—
Jest because it's June—June—June!

SCENE IN VERSE AND PROSE

CARRIE

Julie, do you like him?

JULIE
(Dreaming)

I dunno.

CARRIE

Did you like it when he talked to you today?
When he put you on the carousel, that way?
Did you like that?

JULIE

'D ruther not say.

CARRIE

You're a queer one, Julie Jordan!
You are quieter and deeper than a well,
And you never tell me nothin'—

JULIE

There's nothin' that I keer t' choose t' tell!

CARRIE

You been actin' most peculiar;
Ev'ry mornin' you're awake ahead of me,
Alw'ys settin' by the winder—

86

JULIE

I like to watch the river meet the sea.

CARRIE

When we work in the mill, weavin' at the loom,
Y' gaze absent-minded at the roof,
And half the time yer shuttle gets twisted in the threads
Till y' can't tell the warp from the woof—

JULIE
(*Looking away and smiling.*
She knows it's true.)
'T ain't so!

CARRIE

You're a queer one, Julie Jordan,
You won't ever tell a body what you think.
You're as tight-lipped as an oyster,
And as silent as an old Sahaira Spink!

JULIE

Spinx.

CARRIE

Huh?

JULIE

Spinx.

CARRIE

Uh-uh. Spink.

JULIE

Y' spell it with an *x*.

87

CARRIE

That's only when there's more than one.

JULIE
(*Outbluffed*)

Oh.

CARRIE
(*Looking sly*)

Julie, I been bustin' t' tell *you* somethin' lately.

JULIE

Y' hev?

CARRIE

Reason I didn't keer t' tell you before was 'cause you
didn't hev a feller of yer own. Now y' got one, I ken tell
y' about mine.

JULIE

I'm glad you got a feller, Carrie. What's his name?

CARRIE
(*Now she sings, almost reverently*)

His name is Mister Snow,
And an upstandin' man is he.
He comes home ev'ry night in his round-bottomed boat
With a net full of herring from the sea.
An almost perfect beau,
As refined as a girl could wish,
But he spends so much time in his round-bottomed boat
That he can't seem to lose the smell of fish.

88

The fust time he kissed me, the whiff of his clo'es
Knocked me flat on the floor of the room;
But now that I love him, my heart's in my nose,
And fish is my fav'rite perfume.
Last night he spoke quite low,
And a fair-spoken man is he,
And he said, "Miss Pipperidge, I'd like it fine
If I could be wed with a wife.
And, indeed, Miss Pipperidge, if you'll be mine,
I'll be yours fer the rest of my life."
Next moment we were promised
And now my mind's in a maze,
Fer all I ken do is look forward to
That wonderful day of days . . .

When I marry Mister Snow,
The flowers'll be buzzin' with the hum of bees,
The birds'll make a racket in the churchyard trees,
When I marry Mister Snow.
Then it's off to home we'll go,
And both of us'll look a little dreamy-eyed,
A-drivin' to a cottage by the oceanside
Where the salty breezes blow.
He'll carry me 'cross the threshold,
And I'll be as meek as a lamb.
Then he'll set me on my feet,
And I'll say, kinda sweet:
"Well, Mister Snow, here I am!"

Then I'll kiss him so he'll know
That ev'rythin'll be as right as right ken be,
A-livin' in a cottage by the sea with me,
For I love that Mister Snow—
That young, seafarin', bold and darin',
Big, bewhiskered, overbearin' darlin', Mister Snow!

TWO LITTLE PEOPLE

You can't hear a sound—not the turn of a leaf,
Nor the fall of a wave, hittin' the sand.
The tide's creepin' up on the beach like a thief,
Afraid to be caught stealin' the land.
> On a night like this I start to wonder what life
> is all about.
> And I always say two heads are better than one,
> to figger it out.

> > There's a helluva lot o' stars in the sky,
> > And the sky's so big the sea looks small,
> > And two little people—
> > You and I—
> > We don't count at all.
> > There's a feathery little cloud floatin' by
> > Like a lonely leaf on a big blue stream.
> > And two little people—you and I—
> > Who cares what we dream?

IF I LOVED YOU

If I loved you,
Time and again I would try to say
All I'd want you to know.
If I loved you,
Words wouldn't come in an easy way—
Round in circles I'd go.
Longin' to tell you, but afraid and shy,
I'd let my golden chances pass me by.
Soon you'd leave me,
Off you would go in the mist of day,
Never, never to know
How I loved you—
If I loved you.

*WHEN YOU WALK DOWN
THE AISLE

When you walk down the aisle
All the heads will turn.
What a rustlin' of bonnets there'll be!
And you'll try to smile,
But your cheeks will burn,
And your eyes'll get so dim you ken hardly see.
With your orange blossoms quiverin' in your hand,
You will stumble to the spot where the parson is.
Then your finger will be ringed with a golden band,
And you'll know the feller's yours and you are his.

* *Fragment from* CAROUSEL

BLOW HIGH, BLOW LOW

The people who live on land
Are hard to understand—
When you're lookin' for fun they clap you into jail!
So I'm shippin' off to sea,
Where life is gay and free
And a feller can flip
A hook in the hip of a whale.

Blow high, blow low!
A-whalin' we will go!
We'll go a-whalin', a-sailin' away.
Away we'll go,
Blow me high and low!
For many and many a long, long day,
For many and many a long, long day!

It's wonderful just to feel
Your hands upon a wheel
And to listen to wind a-whistlin' in a sail,
Or to climb aloft and be
The very first to see
A chrysanthemum spout come out o' the snout of a
     whale.

94

Blow high, blow low!
A-whalin' we will go!
We'll go a-whalin', a-sailin' away.
Away we'll go,
Blow me high and low!
For many and many a long, long day,
For many and many a long, long day!

A-rockin' upon the sea,
Your boat will seem to be
Like a dear little baby in her bassinet,
For she hasn't learned to walk
And she hasn't learned to talk,
And her little behind
Is kind of inclined to be wet!

Blow high, blow low!
A-whalin' we will go!
We'll go a-whalin', a-sailin' away.
Away we'll go,
Blow me high and low!
For many and many a long, long day,
For many and many a long, long day!

SOLILOQUY

I wonder what he'll think of me!
I guess he'll call me
"The old man."
I guess he'll think I can lick
Ev'ry other feller's father—
Well, I can!

I bet that he'll turn out to be
The spit an' image
Of his dad,
But he'll have more common sense
Than his puddin'-headed father
Ever had.

I'll teach him to wrassle,
And dive through a wave
When we go in the mornin's for our swim.
His mother can teach him
The way to behave,
But she won't make a sissy out o' him—
Not him!
Not my boy!
Not Bill . . .
Bill!

My boy, Bill!
(I will see that he's named
After me,
I will!)
My boy, Bill—
He'll be tall
And as tough
As a tree,
Will Bill.
Like a tree he'll grow,
With his head held high
And his feet planted firm on the ground,
And you won't see no-
body dare to try
To boss him or toss him around!
No pot-bellied, baggy-eyed bully'll toss him
      around!

I don't give a damn what he does
As long as he does what he likes.
He can sit on his tail
Or work on a rail
With a hammer, a-hammerin' spikes.

He can ferry a boat on the river
Or peddle a pack on his back
Or work up and down

97

The streets of a town
With a whip and a horse and a hack.

He can haul a scow along a canal,
Run a cow around a corral,
Or maybe bark for a carousel—
(Of course it takes talent to do that well.)

He might be a champ of the heavyweights
Or a feller that sells you glue,
Or President of the United States—
That'd be all right, too.

(His mother'd like that. But he wouldn't be
            President unless he wanted to be!
            Not Bill!)
            My boy, Bill—
            He'll be tall
            And as tough
            As a tree,
            Will Bill!
            Like a tree he'll grow,
            With his head held high,
            And his feet planted firm on the ground,
            And you won't see no-
            body dare to try
            To boss him or toss him around!

No fat-bottomed, flabby-faced, pot-bellied,
     baggy-eyed bastard'll boss him around!

And I'm damned if he'll marry his boss' daughter,
A skinny-lipped virgin with blood like water,
Who'll give him a peck and call it a kiss
And look in his eyes through a lorgnette . . .
Say!
Why am I takin' on like this?
My kid ain't even been born yet! . . .

I can see him
When he's seventeen or so
And startin' in to go
With a girl.

I can give him
Lots o' pointers, very sound,
On the way to get round
Any girl.

I can tell him—
Wait a minute! Could it be?
What the hell! What if he
Is a girl! . . .
Bill!
Oh, Bill! . . .

(What would I do with her? What could I do *for* her?
A bum—with no money!)
You can have fun with a son,
But you got to be a *father*
To a girl! . . .

She mightn't be so bad at that—
A kid with ribbons
In her hair,
A kind o' sweet and petite
Little tintype of her mother—
What a pair!
(I can just hear myself braggin' about her!)

My little girl,
Pink and white
As peaches and cream is she.
My little girl
Is half again as bright
As girls are meant to be!
Dozens of boys pursue her,
Many a likely lad
Does what he can to woo her
From her faithful dad.
She has a few
Pink-and-white young fellers of two or three—
But my little girl
Gets hungry ev'ry night

And she comes home to me . . .
My little girl!
My little girl!

I got to get ready before she comes,
I got to make certain that she
Won't be dragged up in slums
With a lot o' bums—
Like me!
She's got to be sheltered and fed, and dressed
In the best that money can buy!
I never knew how to get money,
But I'll try—
By God! I'll try!
I'll go out and make it
Or steal it or take it
Or die!

THIS WAS A
REAL NICE CLAMBAKE

This was a real nice clambake,
We're mighty glad we came.
The vittles we et
Were good, you bet!
The company was the same.
Our hearts are warm,
Our bellies are full,
And we are feelin' prime.
This was a real nice clambake,
And we all hed a real good time.

> Fust come codfish chowder,
> Cooked in iron kettles,
> Onions floatin' on the top,
> Curlin' up in petals.
> Throwed in ribbons of salted pork
> (An old New England trick)
> And lapped it all up with a clamshell,
> Tied on to a bayberry stick.

Oh-h-h—
This was a real nice clambake,
We're mighty glad we came.
The vittles we et

Were good, you bet!
The company was the same.
Our hearts are warm,
Our bellies are full,
And we are feelin' prime.
This was a real nice clambake,
And we all hed a real good time.

Remember when we raked
Them red-hot lobsters
Out of the driftwood fire?
They sizzled and crackled
And sputtered a song,
Fitten fer an angels' choir.
    Fitten fer an angels',
    Fitten fer an angels',
    Fitten fer an angels' choir!
We slit 'em down the back
And peppered 'em good,
And doused 'em in melted butter—
Then we tore away the claws
And cracked 'em with our teeth
'Cause we weren't in the mood to putter! . . .
    Fitten fer an angels',
    Fitten fer an angels',
    Fitten fer an angels' choir!

Then at last come the clams,
Steamed under rockweed
An' poppin' from their shells—
Jest how many of 'em
Galloped down our gullets
We couldn't say oursel's!

Oh-h-h—
This was a real nice clambake,
We're mighty glad we came.
The vittles we et
Were good, you bet!
The company was the same.
Our hearts are warm,
Our bellies are full,
And we are feelin' prime.
This was a real nice clambake,
And we all hed a real good time.

We said it afore—
And we'll say it agen—
We all hed a real good time!

WHAT'S THE USE OF WOND'RIN'?

What's the use of wond'rin'
If he's good or if he's bad,
Or if you like the way he wears his hat?
Oh, what's the use of wond'rin'
If he's good or if he's bad?
He's your feller and you love him—
That's all there is to that.

Common sense may tell you
That the endin' will be sad
And now's the time to break and run away.
But what's the use of wond'rin'
If the endin' will be sad?
He's your feller and you love him—
There's nothin' more to say.

> Somethin' made him the way that he is,
> Whether he's false or true.
> And somethin' gave him the things that are his—
> One of those things is you.

So, when he wants your kisses
You will give them to the lad,
And anywhere he leads you you will walk.

And any time he needs you,
You'll go runnin' there like mad.
You're his girl and he's your feller—
And all the rest is talk.

THE HIGHEST JUDGE
OF ALL

Take me beyond the pearly gates,
Through a beautiful marble hall,
Take me before the highest throne
And let me be judged by the highest Judge of all!

Let the Lord shout and yell,
Let His eyes flash flame,
I promise not to quiver when He calls my name;
Let Him send me to hell,
But before I go,
I feel that I'm entitled to a hell of a show!
Want pink-faced angels on a purple cloud,
Twangin' on their harps till their fingers get red,
Want organ music—let it roll out loud,
Rollin' like a wave, washin' over my head.
Want ev'ry star in heaven
Hangin' in the room,
Shinin' in my eyes
When I hear my doom!

Reckon my sins are good big sins,
And the punishment won't be small;
So take me before the highest throne
And let me be judged by the highest Judge of all.

A MAN WHO THINKS
HE'S GOOD

I never see it yet to fail,
I never see it fail!
A girl who's in love with a virtuous man
Is doomed to weep and wail.

> Stonecutters cut it on stone,
> Woodpeckers peck it on wood:
> There's nothin' so bad fer a woman
> As a man who thinks he's good.

My mother used to say to me:
"When you grow up, my son,
I hope you're a bum like yer father was,
'Cause a good man ain't no fun."

> Stonecutters cut it on stone,
> Woodpeckers peck it on wood:
> There's nothin' so bad fer a woman
> As a man who thinks he's good!

YOU'LL NEVER WALK ALONE

When you walk through a storm
Keep your chin up high
And don't be afraid of the dark.
At the end of the storm
Is a golden sky
And the sweet, silver song of a lark.
Walk on through the wind,
Walk on through the rain,
Though your dreams be tossed and blown.
Walk on, walk on with hope in your heart,
And you'll never walk alone,
You'll never walk alone.

from ALLEGRO

MUSIC BY RICHARD RODGERS

FROM CRADLE TO ALTAR
Sequence of Verses from ALLEGRO, Act I

GRANDMA LOOKS YOU OVER

Starting out so foolishly small,
It's hard to believe you will grow at all.
It's hard to believe that things like you
Can ever turn out to be men,
But I've seen it happen before,
So I know it can happen again.

Food and sleep and plenty of soap,
Molasses and sulphur, and love, and hope—
The winters go by, the summers fly,
And all of a sudden you're men!
I have seen it happen before,
And I know it can happen again.

A FUNNY PLACE TO BE
COMING TO LIFE IN!

It's a funny place.
And those things with the big heads
Don't help to clear things up.

Nobody helps you.
You have to puzzle it out for yourself.

YOU WALK!

Pudgy legs begin to grow long,
And one sunny day, when you're feeling strong,
You straighten a knee and suddenly
You're struck with a daring idea! . . .

One foot, other foot,
One foot, other foot,
One foot, other foot,
One foot, other foot,

Now you can go
Wherever you want,
Wherever you want to go,
One foot out
And the other foot out—
That's all you need to know!

Now you can do
Whatever you want,
Whatever you want to do.

Here you are
In a wonderful world
Especially made for you,
Especially made for you!

Now you can march around the yard,
Shout to all the neighborhood,
Tell the folks you're feeling good
(Folks ought to know when boys feel good).

Now you can imitate a dog,
Chase a bird around a tree,
You can chase a bumblebee
(Once is enough to chase a bee).

Now you can play among the flow'rs,
Grab yourself a hunk o' dirt,
Smudge it on your mother's skirt
(That little dirt won't hurt a skirt).

One foot, other foot,
One foot, other foot,
Now you can do
Whatever you want,
Whatever you want to do.
Here you are
In a wonderful world
Especially made for you,

To walk in, to run in,
To play in the sun in,
For now you can walk,
You taught yourself to walk,
You puzzled it out yourself,
And now you can walk.

Now you can go
Wherever you want,
Wherever you want to go.
One foot out
And the other foot out,
One foot out
And the other foot out,
One foot out
And the other foot out,
And the world belongs to Joe!

YOU MEET DEATH

"These things are nothing for kids." . . .
But it *did* happen to you;
You're a kid,
And yet here you are,
And suddenly you have no grandma.

Death is a sad thing.
People cry and sob,
Grown people.
You haven't seen your father cry.
He just looks kind of angry . . .
Grandma was his mother—
Gosh!
Suppose your mother ever—
Oh, well, *that* isn't going to happen.
Just stop thinking things like that!
Get back to Grandma,
Quick!

THE WINTERS GO BY, THE SUMMERS FLY

The winters go by,
The summers fly,
And soon you're a student in "High"!
And now your clothes are spotlessly clean,
Your head is anointed with brilliantine . . .
You're brimming with hope
But can't quite cope
With problems that vex and perplex,
For you don't quite know how to treat
The bewild'ringly opposite sex.

What do you suppose Jenny would do if
you kissed her?
Jenny is so innocent, so frail!
You could crush her in your strong, manly
arms . . .
But that wouldn't be right.
Besides, she might get sore—
Might yell, and wake up her old man!

(Poor Joe!
The older you grow,
The harder it is to know
What to think,
⠀⠀⠀⠀⠀What to do,
⠀⠀⠀⠀⠀⠀⠀⠀⠀Where to go!)

Heigh-ho! It would have been nice . . .
Think about it as you walk home.
Make believe you did it,
And make out she wasn't mad
When you kissed her.
Gee, wouldn't it be wonderful
If girls liked it too!

COLLEGE

It's a darn nice campus,
With ivy on the walls,
Friendly maples
Outside the lecture halls,
A new gymnasium,
A chapel with a dome—
It's a darn nice campus . . .
And I wish I were home . . .

It's a darn nice campus,
I'm going to like it fine!
Darn cute coeds,
They have a snappy line;
Darn nice fellers,
As far as I can tell—
It's a darn nice campus . . .
And I'm lonely as hell!

It's a darn nice campus,
With ivy on the walls,
Friendly maples
Outside the lecture halls.
I like my roommate,
And you would like him too—
It's a darn nice campus
But I'm lonely for you.

119

LOVE!

You are never away
From your home in my heart;
There is never a day
When you don't play a part
In a word that I say
Or a sight that I see—
      You are never away,
      And I'll never be free.

You're the smile on my face,
Or a song that I sing,
You're a rainbow I chase
On a morning in spring;
You're a star in the lace
Of a wild willow tree—
      In the green, leafy lace
      Of a wild willow tree.

But tonight you're no star,
Nor a song that I sing;
In my arms, where you are,
You are sweeter than spring;
In my arms, where you are,
Clinging closely to me,
      You are lovelier, by far,
      Than I dreamed you could be—

You are lovelier, my darling,
Than I dreamed you could be!

AND SO—

What a lovely day for a wedding!
Not a cloud to darken the sky.
It's a treat to meet at a wedding,
To laugh and to gossip and to cry.

> (What can he see in her?)
> (What can she see in him?)
> (The Brinkers all are stinkers!)
> (All the Taylor crowd is grim!)

THE BEST MAN MEDITATES

It may be a good idea for Joe,
But it wouldn't be good for me
To sit in a mortgaged bungalow
With my little ones on my knee.

121

I'd much rather go and blow my dough
On a casual chickadee.
I don't want a mark that I'll have to toe;
My toe can go where it wants to go;
It wants to go where the wild girls grow
In extravagant quantity.
To bask in the warm and peaceful glow
Of connubial constancy
May be awfully good for good old Joe
But it wouldn't be good for me.

THE ORGAN PEALS

Let the church light up with glory
That belongs to every bride and groom,
May the first bright day of their story
Be a flower that will ever bloom.

> *What happens in a church*
> *During the wedding march?*
> *What suddenly rises in our hearts and hurts us?*
> *Is it the effect of the music?*
> *Or is it the sight of two lovers,*
> *Two lovers,*
> *Looking like two very serious children?*

"DEARLY BELOVED,

We are gathered together here in the sight of
God, and in the face of this company, to join
together this man and this woman in holy matrimony."

A change has come over us.
The simple words,
The commonplace words,
And the two serious children listening—
A change has come over us!
The whispered jokes,
The "cracks" that seemed funny
A few moments ago,
Aren't funny any more.
This is no time for the humorous skeptic
Or the gloomy prophet.
This is a time for hope.
These children desperately
Need our hope!

Two more lovers
Were married today.
Wish them well! Wish them well! Wish them well!
Brave and happy,
They start on their way,
Wish them well! Wish them well! Wish them well!
They have faith in the future

123

And joy in their hearts;
If you look in their eyes
You can tell
How brave and happy
And hopeful are they . . .
Wish them well! Wish them well! Wish them well!

A FELLOW NEEDS A GIRL

A fellow needs a girl
To sit by his side
At the end of a weary day,
To sit by his side
And listen to him talk
And agree with the things he'll say.

A fellow needs a girl
To hold in his arms
When the rest of his world goes wrong,
To hold in his arms
And know that she believes
That her fellow is wise and strong.

When things go right
And his job's well done,
He wants to share
The prize he's won.
(If no one shares,
And no one cares,
Where's the fun
Of a job well done
Or a prize you've won?)

A fellow needs a home,
His own kind of home,
But to make this dream come true
A fellow needs a girl,
His own kind of girl . . .
My kind of girl is you.

MONEY ISN'T EV'RYTHING!

Money isn't everything—
What can money buy?
An automobile, so you won't get wet;
Champagne, so you won't get dry.
Money isn't everything—
What have rich folks got?
A Florida home, so you won't get cold;
A yacht so you won't get hot;
An orchid or two,
So you won't feel blue
If you have to go out at night;
And maybe a jar
Of caviar,
So your appetite won't be light.
Oil tycoon and cattle king,
Radio troubadour,
Belittle the fun that their fortunes
            bring
And tell you that they are sure
Money isn't everything!

Money *isn't* everything,
Money isn't everything
Unless you're very poor!

127

Can money make you honest?
Can it teach you right from wrong?
Can money keep you healthy?
Can it make your muscles strong?
Can money make your eyes get red,
The way they get from sewing?
Can money make your back get sore,
The way it gets from mowing?
Can money make your hands get rough,
As washing dishes does?
Can money make you smell the way
That cooking fishes does?
It may buy you gems and fancy clothes
And juicy steaks to carve,
But it cannot build your character
Or teach you how to starve!

Money isn't everything—
If you're rich, you pay
Elizabeth Arden to do your face
The night you attend a play.
Feeling like the bloom of spring,
Down the aisle you float,
A Tiffany ring, and a Cartier string
Of pearls to adorn your throat.
Your Carnegie dress
Will be more or less
Of a handkerchief round your hip,

Sewed on to you so
That your slip won't show—
And whatever you show won't slip.
To your creamy shoulders cling
Ermines white as snow.
Then on to cafés where they sway and swing,
You go with your wealthy beau.
There you'll hear a crooner sing:
"Money isn't everything!"

Money *isn't* everything,
As long as you have dough!

COCKTAIL PARTY

Yatata, yatata, yatata, yatata,
Yatata, yatata, yatata, yatata,

Busy!
Busy!
I'm busy as a bee!
I start the day at half-past one.
When I am finished phoning
It's time to dress for tea.
Nothing I have to do gets done!

> (The deep-thinking gentlemen and ladies
> Who keep a metropolis alive
> Drink cocktails
> And knock tails
> Ev'ry afternoon at five.)

Yatata, yatata, yatata, yatata,
Yatata, yatata, yatata, yatata,

Doctor,
Doctor,
I need another shot!
(The shots he gives are too divine!

He fills a little needle and he gives you all it's got.
Your fanny hurts, but you feel fine.)

Broccoli, Hogwash, Balderdash,
Phoney, Baloney, Tripe, and Trash!
Goodness knows where the day has gone!
The years of a life are quickly gone,
But the talk, talk, talk goes on and on
And on and on and on—
The prattle and the tattle,
The gab and the gush,
The chatter and the patter,
And the twaddle and the tush
Go on and on and on and on and on.

THE GENTLEMAN IS A DOPE

The boss gets on my nerves;
I've got a good mind to quit.
I've taken all I can;
It's time to get up and git,
And move to another job
Or maybe another town.
The gentleman burns me up,
The gentleman gets me down.

The gentleman is a dope,
A man of many faults,
A clumsy Joe
Who wouldn't know
A rhumba from a waltz.
The gentleman is a dope,
And not my cup of tea.
          (Why do I get in a dither?
          He doesn't belong to me.)

The gentleman isn't bright,
He doesn't know the score;
A cake will come,
He'll take a crumb
And never ask for more.

The gentleman's eyes are blue,
But little do they see.
        (Why am I beating my brains out?
        He doesn't belong to me.)

                He's somebody else's problem;
                She's welcome to the guy!
                She'll never understand him
                Half as well as I.

The gentleman is a dope,
He isn't very smart.
He's just a lug
You'd like to hug
And hold against your heart.
The gentleman doesn't know
How happy he could be.
    (Look at me, crying my eyes out
    As if he belonged to me . . .
    He'll never belong to me.)

ALLEGRO

Our world is for the forceful
And not for sentimental folk,
But brilliant and resourceful
And paranoiac gentle folk.
(Not soft and sentimental folk!)

"Allegro," a musician
Would so describe the speed of it,
The clash and competition
Of counterpoint.
(The need of it?
We cannot prove the need of it.)

We know no other way
Of living out a day.
Our music must be galloping and gay.
We muffle all the undertones,
The minor blood-and-thunder tones;
The overtones are all we care to play.
Hysterically frantic,
We are stubbornly romantic
And doggedly determined to be gay!

Brisk, lively,
Merry and bright—
Allegro!
Same tempo
Morning and night—
Allegro!
Don't stop, whatever you do,
Do something dizzy and new,
Keep up the hullabaloo!
Allegro! Allegro! Allegro! Allegro! Allegro!

    We spin and we spin and we spin and
       we spin,
    Playing a game no one can win.
    The men who corner wheat,
    The men who corner gin,
    The men who rule the air waves,
    The denizens of din—
    They spin and they spin,
    They spin and they spin.
    The girls who dig for gold
    And won't give in for tin,
    The lilies of the field,
    So femininely thin,
    They toil not, they toil not,
    But oh, how they spin!
    Oh, how they spin!
    Oh, how they spin!

May's in love with Kay's husband,
He's in love with Sue.
Sue's in love with May's husband,
What are they to do?
Tom's in love with Tim's wife,
She's in love with Sam.
Sam's in love with Tom's wife,
So they're in a jam.

They are smart little sheep
Who have lost their way,
Blah! Blah! Blah!

Brisk, lively,
Merry and bright—
Allegro!
Same tempo
Morning and night—
Allegro!
Don't stop, whatever you do,
Do something dizzy and new,
Keep up the hullabaloo!
Allegro! Allegro! Allegro! Allegro! Allegro!

from SOUTH PACIFIC

MUSIC BY RICHARD RODGERS

A WONDERFUL GUY

I expect every one
Of my crowd to make fun
Of my proud protestations of faith in romance,
And they'll say I'm naïve
As a babe to believe
Any fable I hear from a person in pants.

Fearlessly I'll face them and argue their doubts away.
Loudly I'll sing about flowers and spring.
Flatly I'll stand on my little flat feet and say,
Love is a grand and a beautiful thing!
I'm not ashamed to reveal
The world-famous feeling I feel.

I'm as corny as Kansas in August,
I'm as normal as blueberry pie.
No more a smart
Little girl with no heart,
I have found me a wonderful guy.
I am in a conventional dither
With a conventional star in my eye,
And you will note
There's a lump in my throat
When I speak of that wonderful guy.

I'm as trite and as gay
As a daisy in May,
A cliché coming true!
I'm bromidic and bright
As a moon-happy night
Pouring light on the dew.
I'm as corny as Kansas in August,
High as a flag on the Fourth of July!
If you'll excuse
An expression I use,
I'm in love,
I'm in love,
I'm in love,
I'm in love,
I'm in love with a wonderful guy!

A COCKEYED OPTIMIST

When the sky is a bright canary yellow
I forget ev'ry cloud I've ever seen—
So they call me a cockeyed optimist,
Immature and incurably green!

I have heard people rant and rave and bellow
That we're done and we might as well be dead—
But I'm only a cockeyed optimist,
And I can't get it into my head.

> I hear the human race
> Is falling on its face
> And hasn't very far to go,
> But ev'ry whippoorwill
> Is selling me a bill
> And telling me it just ain't so!

I could say life is just a bowl of jello
And appear more intelligent and smart,
But I'm stuck, like a dope,
With a thing called hope,
And I can't get it out of my heart!
$\qquad\qquad$ Not this heart!

SOME ENCHANTED EVENING

Some enchanted evening
You may see a stranger,
You may see a stranger
Across a crowded room.
And somehow you know,
You know even then,
That somewhere you'll see her again and again.

Some enchanted evening
Someone may be laughing,
You may hear her laughing
Across a crowded room—
And night after night,
As strange as it seems,
The sound of her laughter will sing in your dreams.

Who can explain it?
Who can tell you why?
Fools give you reasons—
Wise men never try.

Some enchanted evening,
When you find your true love,
When you feel her call you

Across a crowded room—
Then fly to her side
And make her your own,
Or all through your life you may dream all alone.

Once you have found her,
Never let her go.
Once you have found her,
Never let her go!

THERE IS NOTHIN'
LIKE A DAME

We got sunlight on the sand,
We got moonlight on the sea,
We got mangoes and bananas
You can pick right off a tree,
We got volleyball and ping-pong
And a lot of dandy games—
What ain't we got?
We ain't got dames!

We get packages from home,
We get movies, we get shows,
We get speeches from our skipper
And advice from Tokyo Rose,
We get letters doused wit' poifume,
We get dizzy from the smell—
What don't we get?
You know damn well!

We have nothin' to put on a clean white suit for.
What we need is what there ain't no substitute for.

There is nothin' like a dame—
Nothin' in the world!

144

There is nothin' you can name
That is anythin' like a dame.

We feel restless,
We feel blue,
We feel lonely and, in brief,
We feel every kind of feelin'
But the feelin' of relief.
We feel hungry as the wolf felt
When he met Red Riding Hood—
What don't we feel?
We don't feel good!

Lots of things in life are beautiful, but, brother,
There is one particular thing that is nothin' whatsoever
        in any way, shape, or form like any other.

There is nothin' like a dame—
Nothin' in the world!
There is nothin' you can name
That is anythin' like a dame.

Nothin' else is built the same!
Nothin' in the world
Has a soft and wavy frame
Like the silhouette of a dame.
There is absolutely nothin' like the frame of a dame!

So suppose a dame ain't bright,
Or completely free from flaws,
Or as faithful as a bird dog,
Or as kind as Santa Claus—
It's a waste of time to worry
Over things that they have not;
Be thankful for
The things they got!

There is nothin' like a dame—
Nothin' in the world.
There is nothin' you can name
That is anythin' like a dame.

There are no books like a dame
And nothin' looks like a dame.
There are no drinks like a dame
And nothin' thinks like a dame,
Nothin' acts like a dame
Or attracts like a dame.
There ain't a thing that's wrong with any man here
That can't be cured by puttin' him near
A girly, womanly, female, feminine dame!

BALI HA'I

Most people live on a lonely island,
Lost in the middle of a foggy sea.
Most people long for another island,
One where they know they would like to be.

Bali Ha'i
May call you,
Any night,
Any day.
In your heart
You'll hear it call you:
"Come away,
Come away."

Bali Ha'i
Will whisper
On the wind
Of the sea:
"Here am I,
Your special island!
Come to me,
Come to me.

"Your own special hopes,
Your own special dreams,
Bloom on the hillside
And shine in the streams.

"If you try,
You'll find me
Where the sky
Meets the sea;
Here am I,
Your special island!
Come to me,
Come to me!

"Bali Ha'i,
  Bali Ha'i,
    Bali Ha'i.

"Someday you'll see me,
Floating in the sunshine,
My head sticking out
From a low-flying cloud;
You'll hear me call you,
Singing through the sunshine,
Sweet and clear as can be,
Come to me,
Here I am,
Come to me!"

148

Bali Ha'i
Will whisper
On the wind
Of the sea:
"Here am I,
Your special island!
Come to me,
Come to me.

"Bali Ha'i,
    Bali Ha'i,
        Bali Ha'i."

YOUNGER THAN SPRINGTIME

I touch your hand,
And my arms grow strong,
Like a pair of birds
That burst with song.
My eyes look down
At your lovely face,
And I hold the world
In my embrace.

Younger than springtime are you,
Softer than starlight are you;
Warmer than winds of June are the gentle lips you
  gave me.
Gayer than laughter are you,
Sweeter than music are you;
Angel and lover, heaven and earth,
                  Are you to me.
And when your youth and joy invade my arms
And fill my heart, as now they do,
Then, younger than springtime am I,
Gayer than laughter am I,
Angel and lover, heaven and earth,
                  Am I with you.

HAPPY TALK

Happy talk,
Keep talkin' happy talk,
Talk about things you'd like to do.
You gotta have a dream;
If you don't have a dream,
How you gonna have a dream come true?

Talk about a moon
Floatin' in de sky,
Lookin' like a lily on a lake;
Talk about a bird
Learnin' how to fly,
Makin' all de music he can make—

Happy talk,
Keep talkin' happy talk,
Talk about things you'd like to do.
You gotta have a dream;
If you don't have a dream,
How you gonna have a dream come true?

Talk about a star
Lookin' like a toy,
Peakin' t'rough de branches of a tree;

Talk about a girl,
Talk about a boy,
Countin' all de ripples on de sea—

Happy talk,
Keep talkin' happy talk,
Talk about things you'd like to do.
You gotta have a dream;
If you don't have a dream,
How you gonna have a dream come true?

Talk about a boy
Sayin' to a girl:
"Golly, baby! I'm a lucky cuss!"
Talk about de girl
Sayin' to de boy:
"You an' me is lucky to be us!"

Happy talk,
Keep talkin' happy talk,
Talk about things you'd like to do.
You gotta have a dream;
If you don't have a dream,
How you gonna have a dream come true?
If you don't talk happy
An' you never have a dream,
Den you'll never have a dream come true.

Three songs that
were withdrawn from:
SOUTH PACIFIC

The sky is a bright canary yellow,
And the sea is a robin's-egg blue.
It makes you wish,
When you fall asleep,
You will dream about the view.
Bizarre and improbable and pretty
As a page from the fairy-tale books,
It makes you wish
That the world could be
As lovely as it looks.

WILL MY LOVE
COME HOME TO ME?

I wake in the loneliness of sunrise
When the deep-purple heaven turns blue,
And start to pray,
As I pray each day,
That I'll hear some word from you.
I walk in the loneliness of evening,
Looking out on a silver-flaked sea,
And ask the moon:
Oh, how soon, how soon,
Will my love come home to me?

NOW IS THE TIME

Now is the time,
The time to live,
No other time is real.
Yesterday has gone,
Tomorrow is a guess,
Today you can see and feel.
You can feel the wind from the fresh, green sea,
You can smell the salt in the spray.
Now is the time,
The time of your life,
The time of your life is today!

       With heav'nly wine
       From an earth-born vine
       To caress your lips when you're dry,
       With food to eat
       From a field made sweet
       By the sun and the rain from the sky,
       Why flee in fear
       Of a future year
       And accept defeat with a bow?
       While your limbs are sound,
       While your pulses bound,
       You can conquer the future now!

Now!
Now is the time,
The time to act,
No other time will do.
Live and play your part
And give away your heart
And take what the world gives you.
Let your arms get rich on the gold of love,
When the gold of love comes your way.
Now is the time,
The time of your life,
The time of your life is today!

from SHOW BOAT

MUSIC BY JEROME KERN

CAN'T HELP LOVIN'
DAT MAN

Oh, listen, sister,
I love my mister man,
And I can't tell yo' why.
Dere ain't no reason
Why I should love dat man—
It mus' be sumpin' dat de angels done plan.

Fish got to swim, birds got to fly,
I got to love one man till I die—
Can't help lovin' dat man of mine.
Tell me he's lazy, tell me he's slow,
Tell me I'm crazy (maybe I know)—
Can't help lovin' dat man of mine.
When he goes away
Dat's a rainy day,
But when he comes back dat day is fine,
                De sun will shine!
He kin come home as late as kin be,
Home widout him ain't no home to me—
Can't help lovin' dat man of mine.

Mah man is shif'less
An' good for nuthin' too
(He's mah man jes' de same)

He's never round here
When dere is work to do—
He's never round here when dere's workin' to do.
De chimbley's smokin',
De roof is leakin' in,
But he don' seem to care.
He kin be happy
Wid jes' a sip of gin—
Ah even love him when his kisses got gin!

Fish got to swim, birds got to fly,
I got to love one man till I die—
Can't help lovin' dat man of mine.
Tell me he's lazy, tell me he's slow,
Tell me I'm crazy (maybe I know)—
Can't help lovin' dat man of mine.
When he goes away
Dat's a rainy day,
But when he comes back dat day is fine,
                    De sun will shine!
He kin come home as late as kin be,
Home widout him ain't no home to me—
Can't help lovin' dat man of mine!

OL' MAN RIVER

Dere's an ol' man called de Mississippi;
Dat's de ol' man dat I'd like to be!
What does he care if de world's got troubles?
What does he care if de land ain't free?

  Ol' Man River,
  Dat Ol' Man River,
  He mus' know sumpin'
  But don' say nuthin',
  He jes' keeps rollin',
  He keeps on rollin' along.
  He don' plant taters,
  He don' plant cotton,
  An' dem dat plants 'em
  Is soon forgotten,
  But Ol' Man River,
  He jes' keeps rollin' along.
  You an' me, we sweat an' strain,
  Body all achin' an' racked wid pain—
  Tote dat barge!
  Lif' dat bale!
  Git a little drunk,
  An' you land in jail. . . .
  Ah git weary

An' sick of tryin';
Ah'm tired of livin'
An' skeered of dyin',
But Ol' Man River,
He jes' keeps rollin' along.

Colored folks work on de Mississippi,
Colored folks work while de white folks play,
Pullin' dem boats from de dawn to sunset,
Gittin' no rest till de Judgment Day—

Don' look up
An' don' look down—
You don' dast make
De white boss frown.
Bend your knees
An' bow your head,
An' pull dat rope
Until yo' dead.

Let me go 'way from de Mississippi,
Let me go 'way from de white man boss;
Show me dat stream called de river Jordan,
Dat's de ol' stream dat I long to cross.

Ol' Man River,
Dat Ol' Man River,
He mus' know sumpin'
But don' say nuthin',

He jes' keeps rollin',
He keeps on rollin' along.
He don' plant taters,
He don' plant cotton,
An' dem dat plants 'em
Is soon forgotten,
But Ol' Man River,
He jes' keeps rollin' along.
You an' me, we sweat an' strain,
Body all achin' and racked wid pain—
Tote dat barge!
Lif' dat bale!
Git a little drunk,
An' you land in jail. . . .
Ah git weary
An' sick of tryin';
Ah'm tired of livin'
An' skeered of dyin',
But Ol' Man River,
He jes' keeps rollin' along.

YOU ARE LOVE

You are love,
Here in my arms,
Where you belong,
And here you will stay,
I'll not let you away,
I want day after day
With you.
You are spring,
Bud of romance unfurled;
You taught me to see
One truth forever true.
You are love,
Wonder of all the world.
Where you go with me,
Heaven will always be.

*ME AN' MY BOSS

Jes' look at me an' my boss,
Jes' look at me an' my boss!
We's both de same—
We ain't no diff'rent.
I go wherever he goes.
(Dey make me ride in "Jim Crows"—
Excep' for dat
We's both de same.)
Roast beef's his favorite dish,
I likes my taters an' fish—
Excep' for dat
We ain't no diff'rent.
We both git born,
We both grow old an' die,
Him an' I,
Me an' my boss.

*A song written for Paul Robeson to sing in
the London production of SHOW BOAT,
withdrawn in favor of reprise of "Ol' Man
River."

WHY DO I LOVE YOU?

Why do I love you?
Why do you love me?
Why should there be two
Happy as we?
Can you see
The why or wherefore
I should be the one you care for?
You're a lucky boy,
I am lucky too,
All our dreams of joy
Seem to come true—
Maybe that's because you love me . . .
Maybe that's why I love you.

MAKE BELIEVE

Only make believe I love you,
Only make believe that you love me.
Others find peace of mind in pretending—
Couldn't you? Couldn't I? Couldn't we?
Make believe our lips are blending
In a phantom kiss, or two, or three.
Might as well make believe I love you,
For, to tell the truth, I do.

from MUSIC IN THE AIR

MUSIC BY JEROME KERN

I'VE TOLD EV'RY
LITTLE STAR

I've told every little star
Just how sweet I think you are—
Why haven't I told you?
I've told ripples in a brook,
Made my heart an open book—
Why haven't I told you?
Friends ask me
Am I in love,
I always answer "Yes"
(Might as well confess;
If I don't, they guess)
Maybe you may know it too—
Oh, my darling, if you do,
Why haven't you told me, dear?
Why haven't you told me?

171

THERE'S A HILL
BEYOND A HILL

The world can be a wonderful world
When the thrill of adventure comes.
(If you don't like that kind of thing,
Stay home and twiddle your thumbs)
A day can be a wonderful day
When you're out on the open road.
There is no road too long to walk
If you can sing to pass the time.
There is no road too long to walk,
No mountain peak too high to climb!
To climb the highest mountain,
To ford the deepest river,
Will make you feel the zest of life.
Come on and get the best of life,
Come on—
The best of life is farther on!

There's a hill beyond a hill
    Beyond a hill beyond a hill—
If your limbs are young and strong,
Follow along,
Follow along!

There's a dream beyond a dream
   Beyond a dream beyond a dream—
If your heart is young and gay,
Follow along our way!

WHEN THE SPRING
IS IN THE AIR

When the spring is in the air,
I want my fill of the spring,
With all the thrill of the spring
I want to dance.
When I see a happy pair,
I want to fall right in love
And get my own portion of
Romance.
When I hear a pretty song,
I want to sing like a bird,
I want to learn every word
And every rhyme.
I'm susceptible and foolish and young,
But I have a damn good time.

THE SONG IS YOU

I hear music when I look at you,
A beautiful theme of ev'ry dream I ever knew.
Down deep in my heart
I hear it play,
I feel it start,
Then melt away.
I hear music when I touch your hand,
A beautiful melody from some enchanted land.
Down deep in my heart
I hear it say:
Is this the day?
I alone
Have heard this lovely strain,
I alone
Have heard this glad refrain.
Must it be
Forever inside of me?
Why can't I let it go?
Why can't I let you know?
Why can't I let you know the song my heart would sing—
That beautiful rhapsody of love and youth and spring?
The music is sweet,
The words are true,
The song is you.

175

IN EGERN ON THE
TEGERN SEE

In Egern on the Tegern See,
Where we have our home,
We watch the sunset fade away
And melt in the gloam,
And then my man and I,
Beneath a starlit sky,
Look out across the water,
The calm, contented water.
When lights along the shore go out,
My man looks my way,
Then we let one light more go out,
And end one more day.
And while soft breezes bless us
And moonbeams caress us,
We dream in Egern on the Tegern See.

AND LOVE WAS BORN

A warm spring night was stirred by a breeze,
And love was born.
A moon in flight was caught in the trees,
And love was born.
A lark sang out,
And through the mist
There came a sigh
Upon a sigh,
And two young lips were gently kissed
And two young hearts learned to fly. . . .
A shepherd boy awoke from a doze
And blew his horn,
The sun came up and smiled on a rose,
And love was born.

OTHER SONGS

WITH MUSIC BY JEROME KERN

WHY WAS I BORN?

(From *Sweet Adeline*)

Why was I born?
Why am I living?
What do I get?
What am I giving?
Why do I want a thing I daren't hope for?
What can I hope for?
I wish I knew!
Why do I try
To draw you near me?
Why do I cry?
You never hear me.
I'm a poor fool,
But what can I do?
Why was I born
To love you?

CAN I FORGET YOU?

(From the picture *High, Wide and Handsome*)

Can I forget you?
Or will my heart remind me
That once we walked in a moonlit dream?
Can I forget you?
Or will my heart remind me
How sweet you made the moonlight seem?
Will the glory of your nearness
Fade, as moonlight fades in a veil of rain?
Can I forget you,
When ev'ry night reminds me
How much I want you back again?

THE FOLKS WHO LIVE
ON THE HILL

(From *High, Wide and Handsome*)

Someday
We'll build a home on a hilltop high, you and I,
Shiny and new, a cottage that two can fill.
And we'll be pleased to be called
"The folks who live on the hill."
Someday
We may be adding a thing or two, a wing or two,
We will make changes as any family will,
But we will always be called
"The folks who live on the hill."
Our veranda will command a view of meadows green,
The sort of view that seems to want to be seen.
And when the kids grow up and leave us,
We'll sit and look at that same old view, just we two,
Darby and Joan, who used to be Jack and Jill,
The folks who like to be called
What they have always been called,
"The folks who live on the hill."

ALL THE THINGS YOU ARE
(From *Very Warm for May*)

You are the promised kiss of springtime
That makes the lonely winter seem long.
You are the breathless hush of evening
That trembles on the brink of a lovely song.
You are the angel glow
    That lights a star.
The dearest things I know
    Are what you are.
Someday my happy arms will hold you,
And someday I'll know that moment divine
When all the things you are
    Are mine!

THE LAST TIME
I SAW PARIS

A lady known as Paris,
Romantic and charming,
Has left her old companions and faded from view.
Lonely men with lonely eyes are seeking her in vain.
Her streets are where they were,
But there's no sign of her—
She has left the Seine.

The last time I saw Paris,
Her heart was warm and gay.
I heard the laughter of her heart in ev'ry street café.
The last time I saw Paris,
Her trees were dressed for spring
And lovers walked beneath those trees
And birds found songs to sing.
I dodged the same old taxicabs that I had dodged for
          years;
The chorus of their squeaky horns was music to my
          ears.
The last time I saw Paris,
Her heart was warm and gay—
No matter how they change her, I'll remember her
          that way.

I'll think of happy hours
And people who shared them:
Old women selling flowers in markets at dawn,
Children who applauded Punch and Judy in the park,
And those who danced at night and kept their Paris
     bright
Till the town went dark.

  The last time I saw Paris,
  Her heart was warm and gay.
  I heard the laughter of her heart in ev'ry street café.
  The last time I saw Paris,
  Her trees were dressed for spring
  And lovers walked beneath those trees
  And birds found songs to sing.
  I dodged the same old taxicabs that I had dodged for
          years;
  The chorus of their squeaky horns was music to my
          ears.
  The last time I saw Paris,
  Her heart was warm and gay—
  No matter how they change her, I'll remember her
          that way.

SWEETEST SIGHT
THAT I HAVE SEEN

While writing lyrics for *Very Warm for May*
I saw this old couple on Santa Monica beach.
I couldn't proceed with my work on the
play until I had written some recognition of
the pleasure these two happy strangers had
given me. I set the words to a melody written
by Kern several years before.

> I have seen a line of snow-white birds
> Drawn across an evening sky.
> I have seen divine, unspoken words
> Shining in a lover's eye.
> I have seen moonlight on a mountaintop,
> Silver and cool and still.
> I have heard church bells faintly echoing
> Over a distant hill.
> Close enough to beauty I have been,
> And, in all the whole wide land,
> Here's the sweetest sight that I have seen—
> One old couple walking hand in hand.

BANJO SONG

(Written for a picture that was never produced.)

What's my future?
Where am I goin'?
Don't ask me,
Don't ask me.

When I've got the moon
I am wishin' for the sun.
When I'm sittin' in the sun
I am wishin' for the moon.
When I've got no job
I'm as blue as I can be.
When I've got some work to do
I am longin' to be free.

I'm a discontented good-for-nothing sort of
   ne'er-do-well,
Sit around and mope all day until I hear the
   dinner bell,
Sit around and mope all day and dream of what
   can never be.
(It takes so much to satisfy a shiftless guy like me.)

When I've got the moon
I am wishin' for the sun.

When I'm sittin' in the sun
I am wishin' for the moon.
When I've got five bucks
I am wishin' it was ten,
But if I had you to love
Then I'd never wish again!

What's my future?
Where am I goin'?
You tell me,
You tell me.

from CARMEN JONES

MUSIC BY GEORGES BIZET

YOU TALK JUS'
LIKE MY MAW

You talk jus' like my maw,
You even walk jus' like my maw,
An' I know why I'm stuck on you—
It's 'cause I'm jus' like my paw!
Lemme tell you what de Lawd did:
He made you live nex' door,
So we could fall in love
De way my paw an' maw did.

DAT'S LOVE
(Habanera)

Love's a baby dat grows up wild,
An' he don' do what you want him to;
Love ain' nobody's angel child,
An' he won' pay any mind to you.
One man gives me his diamon' stud,
An' I won' give him a cigarette.
One man treats me like I was mud—
An' what I got dat man c'n get.

Dat's love!
    Dat's love!
        Dat's love!
            Dat's love!

You go for me an' I'm taboo,
But if yore hard to get I go for you,
An' if I do, den you are through, boy,
My baby, dat's de end of you,
De end of you!
So take your cue, boy,
Don' say I didn' tell you true.
I tol' you true,
I tol' you truly,
If I love you dat's de end of you!

194

When your lovebird decides to fly
Dere ain' no door dat you c'n close.
She jus' pecks you a quick good-bye
An' flicks de salt from her tail, an' goes.
If you listen, den you'll get taught,
An' here's your lesson for today:
If I chase you, den you'll get caught,
But once I got you I go my way!

Dat's love!
  Dat's love!
    Dat's love!
      Dat's love!

      You go for me an' I'm taboo,
      But if yore hard to get I go for you,
      An' if I do, den you are through, boy.
      My baby, dat's de end of you,
      De end of you!
      So take yore cue, boy,
      Don' say I didn't tell you true.
      I tol' you true,
      I tol' you truly,
      If I love you dat's de end of you.

BEAT OUT DAT RHYTHM ON A DRUM
(Gypsy Song)

I'll tell you why I wanna dance.
It ain' de sweetness in de music—
I like de sweetness in de music,
But dat ain' why I wanna dance.
It's sumpin' thumpin' in de bass,
A bumpin' underneath de music.
Dat bum-bum-bumpin' under music
Is all I need
To start me off.
I don't need nuthin' else to start me off.

Beat out dat rhythm on a drum,
Beat out dat rhythm on a drum,
Beat out dat rhythm on a drum,
An' I don' need no tune at all!
Beat me dat rhythm on a drum,
Beat me dat rhythm on a drum,
Beat me dat rhythm on a drum,
An' I don' need no tune at all!

I feel it beatin' in my bones,
It feel like twen'y millyun tomtoms.
I know dere's twen'y millyun tomtoms
Beatin' way down deep inside my bones.

I feel it beatin' in my heart,
An' den I get a kin' o' dream
An' in my dream it kin' o' seem
Dere's jus' one heart
In all de worl'—
Dere ain't but one big heart for all de worl'.

    Beat out dat rhythm on a drum,
    Beat out dat rhythm on a drum,
    Beat out dat rhythm on a drum,
    Dere's one big heart for all de worl'!
    Beat me dat rhythm on a drum,
    Beat me dat rhythm on a drum,
    Beat me dat rhythm on a drum,
    Dere's one big heart for all de worl'!

An' now dat heart is beatin' fast,
An' dat's a rhythm I kin dance to,
I'm mighty glad I got a chance to,
Wid dat one big heart dat's beatin' fast.
Tomorrow mornin' let it rain,
Tomorrow mornin' let it pour,
Tonight we's in de groove together—
Ain' gonna worry 'bout stormy weather—
Gonna kick ol' trouble out de door!

    Beat out ol' trouble on a drum,
    Beat out ol' trouble on a drum,

Beat out ol' trouble on a drum,
An' kick his carcass through de door!
Beat out dat rhythm on a drum,
Beat out dat rhythm on a drum,
Beat out dat rhythm on a drum,
An' kick ol' trouble out de door!
Kick 'im out de door!
Kick 'im out de door!
Kick 'im out de door!

STAN' UP AN' FIGHT

(Toreador Song)

Thanks a lot!
I'm sure glad to be,
To be where I c'n see
So many friends o' mine.
How've I been doin'?
How've I been doin'?
If you really wanta know de truth,
I'm doin' fine!
Seventeen
Decisions in a row,
An' only five on points;
De res' was all K.O.—
Jackson an' Johnson,
Murphy an' Bronson,
One by one dey come,
An' one by one to dreamland dey go.
How's it done?
You ask me, how's it done?
I got a trainer man
Who taught me all I know.
Sure feels good to have him in my corner,
Hear his voice a-whisp'rin' low:
"Big boy, remember,
You mus' remember . . .

"Stan' up an' fight until you hear de bell,
Stan' toe to toe,
Trade blow fer blow,
Keep punchin' till you make yer punches tell,
Show dat crowd watcher know!
Until you hear dat bell,
Dat final bell,
Stan' up an' fight like hell!"

When you fight
Out in de open air,
In a patch o' light
De ring looks small an' white.
Out in de blackness,
Out in de blackness,
You c'n feel a hun'erd thousan' eyes
Fillin' de night.
Cigarettes
Are blinkin' in de dark,
An' makin' polka dots
Aroun' de baseball park,
People are quiet—
Den dere's a riot!
Someone t'rows a punch
An' plants it right smack on de mark . . .
Somebody's hurt,
You kinda think it's you.
You hang across de ropes—

Da's all you want to do.
Den you look aroun' an' see your trainer's eyes,
Beggin' you to see it through,
Dey say, "Remember,
Big Boy, remember—

"Stan' up an' fight until you hear de bell,
Stan' toe to toe,
Trade blow fer blow,
Keep punchin' till you make yer punches tell,
Show dat crowd watcher know!
Until you hear dat bell,
Dat final bell,
Stan' up an' fight like hell!"

DIS FLOWER

Dis flower dat you threw my way
Has been my frien' by night an' day.
I saw it fade an' lose its bloom,
But still it kept a sweet perfume.
In my cell, through ev'ry darkened hour,
On my lonely eyes lay dis flower,
An' so I'd sleep de whole night through
An' dream of you, an' dream of you.

Den I'd wake up, wid no one near me,
An' talk fo' de jail walls to hear me—
"She ain' de bes',
Dere all de same!
Like all de res',
She jus' a dame."
Den I tol' myse'f I wuz ravin',
Dere wuz jes' one t'ing I wuz cravin'—
It wuzn' food,
It wuzn' dough,
I guess you know
Dat it wuz you.
I only saw you once . . .
Once wouldn' do!

I don' know anythin' about you.
I don' know much about a shinin' star.
Jus' know de worl' is dark widout you—
Dat's all I know . . .
I only wan' you as you are . . .
Dat's how I love you.

DAT OL' BOY

(C A R M E N *cuts the cards.*)

De nine o' spades!

(*She mixes up the cards quickly, then cuts them again.*)

De nine!
Dere he is—de ol' boy,
Plain as kin be!
Death got his han' on me. . . .

It ain' no use to run away f'um dat ol' boy
Ef he is chasin' you.
It's bes' to stan' right up an' look him in de face
When he is facin' you.
Y' gotta be puhpared to go wid dat ol' boy,
No matter what de time.
So I won't fill my pretty eyes wid salty tears—
Cuz I ain' got de time!
I'm gonna run out ev'ry secon' I got lef'
Before he t'rows me down.
I'm gonna laugh an' sing an' use up all my bref
Before he mows me down;
While I kin fly aroun' I'll do my flyin' high—

I'm gonna keep on livin'
Up to de day I die.

(She looks down at the nine of spades.)

De nine! . . . Hello, ol' boy—hello!

MY JOE

How kin I love a man when I know he don' wan' me?
He ain' been good. He ain' been kind.
He gimme up for a ol' roadside woman—
But I cain' drive him from my mind.

My Joe,
He wuz always my Joe.
Dere wuz no one but me—
Joe said dere never could be.
We wuz in love,
An' I reckon we showed it.
F'um de way people talked,
Reckon ev'ryone knowed it.
Kids on de street where we'd go
Useter yell at us:
"Cindy Lou belongs to Joe!"
Lawd! O Lawd, y' know dat dat wuz true,
An' Joey belonged to Cindy Lou.

I is skeered.
O Lawd! I is skeered!
I'se like a leaf dat los' her tree.
I'se alone.
O Lawd! I'se alone!

He got hisse'f anudder woman.
Now she got his arms all aroun' her—
No, Lawd I cain' believe it's so.
No! No! Don' yer let her keep my Joe.
Make him t'row her back where he foun' her!
Joe! Y' said dat both your arms wuz mine—
Remember? Y' said your arms wuz mine.

I'se yo' gal,
I wuz always yo' gal.
Dere wuz no one but me—
You said dere never could be.
We wuz in love,
An' I reckon we showed it.
F'um de way people talked,
Reckon ev'ryone knowed it.
Kids on de street where we'd go
Useter yell at us:
"Cindy Lou belongs to Joe!"
Lawd! O Lawd, look down an' try to see
How you kin make Joe come home to me.

SONGS

WITH MUSIC BY SIGMUND ROMBERG

LOVER, COME BACK TO ME!

(From *New Moon*)

The sky was blue,
And, high above,
The moon was new,
And so was love.
This eager heart of mine was singing:
"Lover, where can you be?"
You came at last,
Love had its day.
That day is past,
You've gone away.
This aching heart of mine is singing:
"Lover, come back to me!"
Rememb'ring every little thing you used to say and do,
I'm so lonely.
Every road I walk along I've walked along with you—
No wonder I am lonely!
The sky is blue,
The night is cold.
The moon is new,
And love is old.
And while I'm waiting here
This heart of mine is singing:
"Lover, come back to me!"

LOVE IS QUITE A
SIMPLE THING
(From *New Moon*)

> Love is quite a simple thing,
> And nothing so bewildering,
> No matter what the poets sing
> In words and phrases lyrical.
> Birds find bliss in every tree,
> And fishes kiss beneath the sea,
> So when love comes to you and me,
> It really ain't no miracle.

Refrain from EAST WIND

> Your two soft arms embrace me,
> And you are mine to hold.
> The moon is on the river,
> And yellow sails are gold.
> Our lives like clouds are flying,
> And men with hopes are dying,
> But two soft arms embrace me,
> And you are mine to hold.
> The moon is on the river,
> And yellow sails are gold.

Refrain from EAST WIND

Don't trust
A man of my type.
A man like me
Can mean no good
To a girl—
A gay deceiver,
A butterfly type,
Without a good redeeming trait.
Don't trust
A man of my type,
Or you will soon regret your fate.
Now that I have warned you,
How about a date?

WHEN I GROW
TOO OLD TO DREAM

(From the picture *The Night Is Young*)

When I grow too old to dream
I'll have you to remember.
When I grow too old to dream
Your love will live in my heart.
So kiss me, my sweet,
And so let us part,
And when I grow too old to dream
That kiss will live in my heart.